Chocolate!

Chocolate!

Rich and luscious recipes for cakes,
cookies, desserts and treats

Kathryn Hawkins

Good Books
Intercourse, PA 17534
800/762-7171
www.GoodBooks.com

This edition copyright © 2008 by Good Books, Intercourse, PA 17534

International Book Number: 978-1-56148-619-9 (paperback edition)
International Book Number: 978-1-56148-620-5 (comb-bound edition)
Library of Congress Catalog Card Number: 2007036749

Text and recipe copyright © 2008 Kathryn Hawkins
Photographs copyright © 2008 New Holland Publishers (UK) Ltd
Copyright © 2008 New Holland Publishers (UK) Ltd

Library of Congress Cataloging-in-Publication Data

Hawkins, Kathryn.
 Chocolate! : rich and luscious recipes for cakes, cookies, desserts, and treats / Kathryn Hawkins.
    p. cm.
 Includes bibliographical references and index.
 ISBN 978-1-56148-619-9 (pbk. : alk. paper)
 ISBN 978-1-56148-620-5 (comb-bound : alk. paper)
 1. Cookery (Chocolate) 2. Desserts. 3. Chocolate.
 I. Title. II. Title: Rich and luscious recipes for cakes, desserts, and treats.
 TX767.C5H29 2008
 641.6'374--dc22
                              2007036749

Editor: Clare Sayer
Copy Editor: Clare Hubbard
Design: Paul Wright
Photography: Stuart West
Food Styling: Katie Rogers
Production: Hema Gohil
Editorial Direction: Rosemary Wilkinson

Reproduction by Pica Digital Pte Ltd, Singapore
Printed and bound in China by C&C Offset Printing Co

Acknowledgments
Thanks, as ever, to friends, family and neighbors who managed to eat cake, after cookie, after muffin, after brownie, after dessert and anything chocolatey that I put in front of them!

Notes
The author and publishers have made every effort to ensure that all instructions given in this book are safe and accurate, but they cannot accept liability for any resulting injury or loss or damage to either property or person, whether direct or consequential and howsoever arising.

Both metric and imperial measures are given in the recipes – follow either set of measures but not a mixture of both as they are not interchangeable.

Oven temperatures are given for conventional ovens. If using a fan oven, reduce the oven temperature by 70°F (20°C).

Due to the slight risk of salmonella, children, the elderly and pregnant women should avoid recipes with lightly cooked or raw eggs.

Medium eggs should be used unless otherwise stated.

Contents

Introduction

Chocolate is as popular as ever, with more varieties available today than ever before. I've never met anyone who doesn't like chocolate. In my experience, you either love it or you *really* love it! For me, the best way to enjoy chocolate is in the form of a piece of gooey chocolate fudge cake, washed down with a cup of coffee. It's an indulgent, sweet treat, to which nothing else comes remotely close.

As children, my brother and I were allowed chocolate only on special occasions and I still regard it as such today. When my grandparents came to visit us, they always brought us chocolate, but we were allowed to indulge only after we finished all our lunch. Humorously enough, our lunch was always gobbled down! When we spent our pocket money on sweets, I remember that milk or white chocolate mice and chocolate buttons covered in sprinkles were a "must have," and an ice-cream cone just wasn't the same without a chocolate treat stuck in the top. Some of my happiest childhood days were a special outing followed by a chocolate reward for good behavior. We have a marvelous photograph of my brother typifying such an occasion – his mouth and hands are smothered in chocolate and he looks blissfully happy, his face lit up with a broad chocolatey smile.

The great thing about chocolate for me, as a food writer, is that it's so versatile. Apart from being a delicious morsel to eat and enjoy on its own, chocolate can be used for baking; making candy, hot and cold puddings, sauces, and frostings; piping decorations; or flavoring drinks – the list is endless. It's an excellent subject for a cookbook because you can make so many things with it, as you will find out. Chocolate has a fascinating history and, as you'll discover, an almost mythical story. It is also reputed to have all sorts of effects on the body and psyche, so I've included a bit of chocolate trivia for you to enjoy. You'll find all you need to know about using chocolate in your cooking, as well as notes on the different varieties

on the market today and lots of ideas for using chocolate to further enhance your creations. The chapters are divided by kinds of dessert for easy reference, with plenty of traditional favorites alongside more contemporary ideas. I use a wide range of chocolate varieties in my recipes from the lightest, creamiest white to the darkest, most intense, unsweetened chocolate. On pages 169-170, you'll find a list of famous chocolatiers who have made a living out of their love of chocolate. Their work is highly innovative, and they use the best quality chocolate available and subsequently can demand high prices for their product. It's worth sampling some of their creations – pure bliss!

It's been great fun tasting and cooking with all the different types of chocolate and very interesting working out which varieties suit specific recipes and flavorings. I hope you enjoy trying out my recipes for yourself, friends and family. And now I need to go on a diet...!

The story of chocolate

Cocoa originates in the New World. The Mexican Olmec people were the first to cultivate the cocoa tree, and it was later adopted by the Mayans sometime before 600 BC. The Mayans grew cocoa in Central America and, in turn, traded it to the Aztecs. The Aztecs developed cocoa as a product by roasting and grinding the beans and turning it into a drink. It was such a valuable commodity to them that they used the beans as currency.

The wider world learned of this great product from Christopher Columbus who, on his fourth voyage in 1502, brought some back to Spain. He and his entourage told stories of the Aztecs' rituals and recipes. The Aztec emperor, Montezuma, would indulge in a bitter chocolate drink flavored with chillies and spices, served in gold goblets, which he took as an aphrodisiac. The drink was called xocolatl, meaning "bitter water." Aztec soldiers and dignitaries would drink it after a meal by grinding a block of cocoa into hot water. Although bitter-tasting, it was reported as being refreshing and satisfying. The Aztec flavorings were soon adopted by the Spanish, and throughout Europe cocoa concoctions began to include sugar, nuts, spices and flower waters.

The first European cocoa factory opened in Spain in 1580, and it produced a spicy paste. In France and England, the added ingredients were stripped back to vanilla and sugar only, and by the late seventeenth century, this simple mixture was sold as a hot drink made with milk in the trendy Parisian and London coffee houses of the day. The first French factory opened in Bayonne in the eighteenth century and sold cocoa to companies in Paris and beyond.

The Spanish spread cocoa cultivation to Africa. From Mexico, cocoa was exported to the Philippines and cultivation was extended throughout the East Indies by the Dutch. Colonial Americans obtained cocoa from the West Indies and by the late seventeenth century it was enjoyed there as a hot drink. Cocoa production began in North America in 1765 when Dr. James Baker opened a small mill in Massachusetts and entered the business. In 1828 in the Netherlands, Van Houten unveiled a press that extracted more cocoa butter from the beans than was possible before. The resulting cocoa was smoother and finer and was easier to mix with liquid; it was called Dutch cocoa powder. The press led to the development of techniques we associate today with chocolate-making and by the mid-1800s, the first solid chocolate bars were developed in England by the Cadbury brothers and Fry & Sons, and the chocolate industry was born. In 1876, Daniel Peter of Switzerland presented the first milk chocolate bar to the world, and a couple of years later, another Swiss producer, Lindt, started making finer quality chocolates.

At the turn of the twentieth century in the United States, Milton Hershey invented the Hershey bar and pointed the way for other manufacturers to follow. Throughout the century, chocolate was increasingly consumed by the masses, turning chocolate into a multi-billion dollar global industry. Chiefly, the majority of the chocolate eaten was in the form of sweetened candy bars, but Lindt continued producing finer chocolate and catered to the more sophisticated palate.

By the 1970s, interest in darker chocolate for cooking and eating grew, along with a fascination for discovering the roots of chocolate and seeking out original Aztec flavorings.

Today chocolate has reached new heights as a gourmet food. It is promoted by specialist clubs and societies; tastings are conducted and chocolate is appreciated in the same way as fine wine. Professional chocolatiers will listen for the sharp "snapping" sound of good quality chocolate, and their noses will detect notes of flower essences, fruits, balsam and green tea. The Internet has provided easy access to chocolates from all over the world, enabling us to taste the most delicious creations, in often outrageous shapes, flavored with fine liqueurs, champagne and decorated with gold leaf. (See page 169-170 for a list of some of the world's finest chocolate-makers.)

Chocolate is a crowd-wooer and show-stopper, and nothing does that job at a party better than a chocolate fountain. Who can resist the molten, rippling chocolate as it flows seductively? However, for me, it's satisfying to know that any celebration or get-together can still be halted by the arrival of a chocolate cake. I've made chocolate wedding cakes for both my brother and my best friend, and I can remember being showered with compliments from everyone on how lovely it was to have a chocolate cake instead of the more traditional ones. It seems our love for this ancient food grows stronger… let's hope it stays that way.

The feelgood factor

The Aztecs were first to recognize the uplifting properties of cocoa, both as an aphrodisiac and a stimulant. Soon after cocoa was introduced to France, it was used by the medics as a cure for fevers and chest and stomach disorders, and was widely sold in apothecaries in the eighteenth and nineteenth centuries. In the U.K., the Quaker families of Cadbury, Fry, Terry and Rowntree advertised cocoa powder as a healthy alternative to gin, claiming that it was a restorative health tonic for the working classes and not just for the food society's elite. This may seem a bit strange to us today, but these are the foundations for some of our modern-day thoughts and notions about chocolate.

In the twenty-first century, we are bombarded with health reports and conflicting information about the merits of chocolate, so here are some solid facts:

• Cocoa beans, like all beans, are rich in nutrients because they support the germination of a plant. They are rich in the antioxidant vitamin E and the super antioxidants – flavonoids. These help reduce the build-up of blood cholesterol on the artery walls. Although high cocoa solids mean high antioxidants, the addition of milk, sugar or cocoa butter dilutes these properties.

• Cocoa and chocolate are rich in saturated fat which is notorious for raising blood cholesterol. However, the type of saturated fat found in cocoa is one that the body is able to convert into an unsaturated fat that actually lowers the risk of blood clotting which can lead to a heart attack. Once again, this refers to chocolate in its purest form, with a high cocoa content.

• Cocoa and chocolate contain two stimulants – theobromine and caffeine. The former is a weaker stimulant of the nervous system than caffeine. The amount of caffeine found in cocoa and chocolate is significantly lower than in tea and coffee. For example, 1oz (30g) cocoa contains 60mg caffeine; the same amount of unsweetened chocolate

substances that can affect the brain in a similar way to marijuana, and also phenylethylamine, a natural chemical with amphetamine-like effects. However, psychologists have carried out tests on patients who "lust" after chocolate, and have shown that they can be just as satisfied after eating imitations containing no chocolate at all.

• Chocolate is very easy and pleasurable to eat. It melts quickly and smoothly on the tongue, providing great sensory pleasure, stimulating the taste buds and releasing "happy" chemicals in the brain called endorphins. Combine these properties with the energy boost from the sugar and fat content, and this is probably more of an explanation for an individual's cravings and why so many people are seduced by chocolate.

• Because chocolate is rich in fat, and sugar in some varieties, it is high in calories and good for a quick energy boost. It also contains protein and iron. This makes it essential survival food for soldiers and mountaineers.

contains 30mg; milk chocolate contains even less. By comparison, a standard cup of instant coffee has about 80mg caffeine.

• Many people experience cravings for chocolate. It does contain very small amounts of

Types of chocolate

When I was a little girl, in my innocence, I believed that there were only two types of chocolate: chocolate for adults, and chocolate for children. Theirs was semisweet and ours was milk or white – a very simplistic formula but the basic theory was vaguely correct, although I can now see that it was applied when my parents wanted to keep us away from their chocolate!

In reality, chocolate is available in many different forms, from powdered to solid block, in portions for easy baking or more refined bars for eating. All chocolate, even that of the same type, has its own taste due to differences in the location, quality, production and manufacturing of the cocoa beans used. Just like variations in types of tea and coffee, there are several different types of cocoa beans, and these are carefully blended to achieve the best flavor possible. Chocolate manufacturing is a complex process, but it's an interesting journey from the origins of a seed from the cacao tree to the finished product. A brief overview of its production from start to finish follows.

PRODUCTION OF CHOCOLATE
The cacao is an evergreen tree native to Latin America that grows from 20–40 feet (6–12 meters) tall, depending on conditions. It requires shelter and protection as it grows, and this is usually supplied by banana or rubber trees. The flowers grow directly on the tree trunk, but only a few develop into the oval, melon-shaped pods that are either deep yellow or rich red in color. The flowers and pods grow together throughout the year, but the pods are harvested only twice a year. When the pods are ripe, they are collected, split and the contents scraped out. The seeds or beans and surrounding pulp are left in the sun to help them ferment and, in turn, develop a good flavor. Once this has happened, the beans are dried and exported for processing.

On arrival at the factory, the beans are cleaned and then roasted to develop the flavor further and reduce the moisture content. The husks are removed, which leaves only the kernels or nibs – these are the vital parts of chocolate and cocoa manufacturing. They are ground into a paste and the heat produced by the grinding mechanism at this stage helps release the fat or cocoa butter. Once ground, the resulting chocolate mass becomes liquid and is known as chocolate liquor. When the liquor cools, it solidifies and becomes basic, unsweetened chocolate. It can then be processed further to make cocoa and other types of chocolate.

COCOA POWDER

Chocolate liquor is pressed further to exude more cocoa butter, and then the residue is ground down to make the dry powder we know as cocoa. It is unsweetened and has a fat content between 10 and 35 percent. Cocoa is used in baking and desserts and is sifted into mixtures to give a pure, intense chocolate flavor. It can also be mixed with sugar and hot milk to make a rich drink.

HOT CHOCOLATE MIX

Hot chocolate mix or chocolate powder is specifically designed for mixing with hot milk and/or hot water to make a soothing drink or for sprinkling over cakes, desserts and frothy coffee. Some are made from chocolate powder with sugar, emulsifying agents and flavorings added; better quality varieties contain cocoa powder and grated chocolate. Other products also have dried milk powder added and are "instant drinks," requiring only hot water to make them. Because of the increased sugar and lower cocoa content, hot chocolate mix is not a suitable substitute for cocoa powder.

UNSWEETENED/BAKER'S CHOCOLATE

This is cooled chocolate liquor mixed with a quantity of cocoa butter, and can contain up to 95 percent cocoa. It contains no sugar and is therefore very bitter and reddish-brown in color. It grates and melts well and, like cocoa, it gives a full chocolate flavor. It is often packaged wrapped in individual 1oz (30g) squares, and is widely available in most supermarkets in North America. If you cannot find this type of chocolate you can either replace it with one of the very high percentage cocoa chocolates, at least 85 percent, (see below), or make your own mixture by combining 3 level Tbsp cocoa powder with ½oz (15g) unsalted butter. This would replace 1oz (30g) unsweetened chocolate. Remember to adjust the sugar quantity in the recipe accordingly, if necessary.

HIGH PERCENTAGE COCOA BITTER CHOCOLATE

Ranging from 85–100 percent cocoa, this type of chocolate is usually available from specialist suppliers, and is designed for the real chocolate connoisseur. It is primarily very bitter and the intense flavor is not for the faint hearted. But if this is your taste, you'll find different varieties described as having specific qualities (much like ground coffee) depending on the beans used and the roasting process. It is glossy, smooth and has a clean "snapping" sound when broken. This type of chocolate is mainly used in cooking for a full, rich flavor, although it is often an expensive alternative to other types.

BITTERSWEET CHOCOLATE

This type of chocolate has lower cocoa solids than those listed previously – usually between 50–78 percent – with sugar added to it. It gives a good flavor and is probably the most widely used variety. It is ideal for desserts and goes well with coffee. This sort of chocolate can be eaten on its own, although it is probably too rich for most people to eat more than a few squares at a time.

SEMISWEET CHOCOLATE

Much more suitable for eating, this is a chocolate with lower cocoa solids and more sugar. All semisweet chocolate sold in the U.S. must contain at least 35–50 percent cocoa solids, and in the European Union it must contain 30 percent, but it may, in effect, have as little as 15 percent chocolate liquor. Often the sugar content is quite high, so this may make it unsuitable for cooking; you will have to adjust the sugar content in the recipe to suit the chocolate's sweetness.

MILK CHOCOLATE

Milk chocolate contains powdered or condensed milk and sugar which makes it sweet, creamy and mild in flavor. It has a lower percentage of cocoa solids –

typically about 20 percent, although richer varieties are available. It is very popular for eating as a treat, and most prepared chocolate confectionery bars are made from this type of chocolate.

WHITE CHOCOLATE

This is not strictly a chocolate because it is not made from cocoa beans. It is made from cocoa butter to which milk, sugar and vanilla have been added. A sign of good quality would be that the chocolate was made with "natural" or "pure" vanilla rather than "flavoring." It has the same texture as other types of chocolate, but is pale yellowy-white in color and tastes very sweet and creamy. It can be used like other chocolate, but it is not really interchangeable with other types. It is often used in conjunction with a darker variety to give color contrast. Special care should be taken when melting white chocolate as it is more sensitive to heat than other varieties (see pages 21 and 22). White chocolate is a favorite treat among children.

FLAVORED CHOCOLATE

There are many varieties of flavored chocolate bars on the market today; some higher-end bars use natural flavors, while others may include artificial flavorings. When it comes to choosing one, it's a matter of personal preference. Flavored chocolate may not melt very well as it is made for eating on its own rather than cooking, but if the chocolate is of good quality it may be used in baking and offers an additional flavor to your chosen recipe. Common flavors include vanilla, coffee, cinnamon, orange and mint.

CHOCOLATE CHIPS, KISSES AND CHUNKS

Available in white, milk and semisweet varieties, these are small pieces of chocolate specially designed for baking and adding to recipes, such as cookies and muffins, or for sprinkling over ice creams and desserts for extra chocolate flavor. They melt easily, but make sure the chocolate is good quality by checking the cocoa solid content. Some products are made without cocoa butter and have vegetable oil and stabilizers added to them instead; they have a different taste and mouth-feel

and are an inferior product, but do offer a firmer set than baking chocolate when used in desserts and sauces. As an alternative, you can chop your preferred bar of chocolate into small pieces and use this instead of the ready-prepared pieces.

COUVERTURE OR COATING CHOCOLATE

This is a high-quality chocolate mainly used by professional chocolate-makers. This type of chocolate requires "tempering" – a process necessary for fine chocolate making (see page 28). Couverture contains a high percentage of cocoa solids which give it the very glossy finish that is an essential mark of excellence. Available in bitter, semisweet, milk and white varieties, it is expensive. Available from specialist suppliers.

COMPOUND CHOCOLATE

Not to be confused with the couverture chocolate, this is an inferior chocolate product made from cocoa solids mixed with vegetable oil and flavorings. It is used for melting, dipping and molding but lacks real chocolate flavor and glossiness. Inexpensive and easy to use, it is available in semisweet, milk and white varieties.

ORGANIC CHOCOLATE

Increasing concern about the quality of food we consume has led to a rise in the production of organic foods, and chocolate and cocoa products are now widely available with this certification. The principle behind organic food is that it should be produced without the use of genetically-modified crops, pesticides and artificial fertilizers. The term "organic" on food labeling is controlled in law by governments or legislative bodies, and any food labeled as such must meet a strict set of standards. It's often a matter of personal choice, but some people say that organic chocolate products taste better, and help

eliminate ingesting artificial chemicals and additives.

FAIRTRADE® CHOCOLATE

The Fairtrade® mark is an independent consumer label that appears on certain products as a guarantee that disadvantaged producers in the developing world are getting a better deal. The producers receive a minimum price that covers the cost of sustainable production and an extra premium that is invested in social or economic development projects. Producers' working conditions are better, and they have more control over their lives as well as the chance to improve life for their family and community. Chocolate and cocoa are products that can be produced in this way, and cocoa is one of the most environmentally-friendly of all crops. Cocoa producers belonging to this scheme can be found in the Dominican Republic, Ghana and Belize. Look for the Fairtrade® label to support the development of this type of production.

CHOCOLATE FOR SPECIAL DIETS

The dietary restrictions that an individual has will determine the type of chocolate he or she can eat. If you have to avoid dairy food, then choose a bitter chocolate variety, or cocoa powder, which has no added milk. For sugar-restricted diets, unsweetened chocolate or a high percentage cocoa chocolate may be suitable in cooking, as would cocoa powder. However, as these products are so bitter, they probably would be intolerable without added sweetness. Carob is often used as a chocolate alternative, but the flavor is more caramel-like. Carob is a bean from a Mediterranean tree but, unlike chocolate, contains little fat and no caffeine. As such, it would be a suitable alternative for someone on a low-fat diet or who is caffeine intolerant. Carob can be obtained in a powder-like cocoa or in bars – with and without sugar, with dairy or soy milk, flavored, or with fruit and nuts.

ENHANCING THE FLAVOR OF CHOCOLATE IN YOUR COOKING

The Aztecs blended cocoa with spices, scented flowers and even chillies. Today, the most widely-used flavoring is vanilla, as it enhances both the aroma and flavor of many chocolate recipes. Spices like cinnamon, nutmeg, allspice and star anise also combine well with chocolate. If you want to try something more exotic, infuse chocolate-laced liquids with lemon grass, kaffir lime and spicy red chilli. The Mexicans add unsweetened chocolate or cocoa powder to rich spicy beef stews to make an intensely-flavored sauce. Fresh basil increases the balsam, pepperiness of bitter chocolate and I've even tried the darkest of chocolates with salty blue cheese – the flavors are strangely similar! In baking and candy-making, popular additions are coffee, caramel, toffee, banana, mint, orange, lime and roasted nuts. If you use dark brown sugar in the mixture for cakes, muffins or brownies, or light brown sugar for cookies, you'll increase the moistness and "gooey" texture of your finished recipe.

CHOOSING AND STORAGE TIPS

Chocolate that is fresh and in tip-top condition should be glossy and unblemished. Avoid any with a grayish tone, white spots or small holes. In general, it is best to keep chocolate in its original wrapping, or in foil, and then in an airtight container. Cocoa powder is best kept in its original container as long as it is airtight. Store in a cool, dry place, about

64°F (18°C) – the kitchen cupboard should be fine – but not in the fridge unless it is very warm. If you do keep chocolate in the fridge, it is likely that a whitish film will appear on the surface, which is the cocoa butter resurfacing. Although it doesn't affect the taste in any way, it does make the chocolate look unattractive.

Unsweetened and bitter chocolate will keep for many months if stored correctly. Semisweet and milk varieties will keep for about a year, and white chocolate for 6–8 months, but always read "best before" date on the packaging to be sure. Humidity will shorten the shelf life of chocolate, and other incorrect storage conditions will cause the chocolate to "bloom." This bloom occurs when the chocolate becomes damp and some of the sugar starts to dissolve. When the chocolate dries off again the sugar is left on the surface, giving it a moldy-white appearance. If chocolate gets too warm, the cocoa butter melts and forms grayish-white areas on the surface when it cools. Although bloom spoils the appearance of the chocolate, it doesn't affect the flavor and the chocolate can still be eaten, but it is probably best used in cooking.

Chocolate techniques

Chocolate is a very versatile ingredient and you can use it to make many attractive decorations that will add flavor and a touch of decadence to finished cakes, desserts and sweet treats. Here are a few ideas to help you get the most from chocolate and a few suggestions for special finishing touches.

MELTING CHOCOLATE

Chocolate melts at blood heat so little heat is required to soften it. The conventional method for melting chocolate on its own requires using a double boiler system. The other method that is now used is heating it in a microwave oven. When melting chocolate with other ingredients, it is often necessary to use the direct heat method (see page 22).

Double boiler

Break the chocolate into pieces and either place in a double boiler saucepan or in a heatproof bowl. Place the boiler top or the bowl over a saucepan of hot water. Make sure that the base of the bowl doesn't touch the water. Gently heat; do not let the water

boil or produce steam. Allow the chocolate to melt – the time this takes will depend on the thickness and the amount of chocolate used. Chocolate retains its shape as it melts, so it will need a gentle stir to make it smooth. Carefully remove the boiler top or bowl from the saucepan and wipe away the water droplets. It is vital that no water gets into the chocolate as it melts as this will cause the chocolate to irreversibly stiffen and separate, rendering it unusable.

Microwave oven
High percentage cocoa or unsweetened chocolate can be melted at 50 percent or medium power in the microwave, while milk and white are better melted on 30 percent or low power. Break the chocolate into pieces and place in a microwave-proof bowl. The time it will take to melt the chocolate will depend on the amount used, its thickness and the power of the oven. As a rough guide: 3½oz (100g) high percentage cocoa chocolate will take about 4 minutes to melt using a 650–700W microwave oven at 50 percent power. The same amount of milk or white chocolate would take the same time at 30 percent power. Adjust time and power according to your oven. Check the chocolate frequently to make sure it isn't burning – white chocolate is especially susceptible to scorching.
NOTE: Chocolate melted in the microwave with liquid or fat may melt more quickly because of the higher fat content of the ingredients, so it is advisable to check more frequently.

Direct heat method
This is used when other ingredients require melting as well, or when a hot amalgam of ingredients is needed – for example, in a hot chocolate sauce. Choose a heavy-based saucepan and melt the ingredients together over a very low heat, stirring frequently, until melted and smooth. Remove from the heat immediately. Don't be tempted to raise the heat, otherwise the contents will burn and spoil.

MARBLING
Marbling different types of chocolate together is one of the most stunning effects. You can either use it to top cakes and bakes (see Triple chocolate millionaire's shortbread on page 86) or make a sheet of marbled chocolate for creating curls, cut-outs or chocolate cases. The basic principle is the same however you use marbled chocolate.

Choose two or three contrasting colors of chocolate and melt in separate bowls (see page 21). Place alternate teaspoonfuls of the melted chocolate on the cake if decorating, or on a board lined with baking parchment if making a sheet of marbled chocolate. Tap the pan on the work surface so that the chocolates merge together, then drag a skewer through the chocolates to create a marbled effect. Tap again to smooth the chocolate and allow to set according to your recipe.

CHOCOLATE CURLS

There are several ways to make curls of chocolate.

Quick curls

Use a thick bar of chocolate that has been stored at room temperature. Hold the chocolate over a large plate or board lined with baking parchment, and use a swivel-headed vegetable peeler to "peel" firmly along the edge of the chocolate, allowing the curls to fall on the plate or parchment. Place on a plate, lined with baking parchment and chill until required.

Caraque curls

Melt the chocolate (see page 21) and spread it in a thin layer onto a marble slab or clean, smooth cutting board. Leave in a cool place until firm, but not hard (try to avoid refrigerating unless it is very warm). Draw a sharp, thin-bladed knife at a slight angle across the chocolate, using a slight sawing movement, scraping

off thin layers to form long thin scrolls. Place on a plate lined with baking parchment and chill until required. This technique takes some practice! Store as for Quick curls (see left).

Chunky curls

Prepare the chocolate as for caraque curls (see left). Drag a cheese slicer over the surface to form thick, curled scrolls. Store as above.

PIPING CHOCOLATE AND PIPED DECORATIONS

Iced cakes can be finished with simple chocolate piping. Melt the chocolate (see page 21) and spoon into a small, ready-made piping bag. Pipe tiny dots, double lines or shapes like hearts and flowers onto small cakes. For a contemporary look for a large cake, pipe the word "chocolate" over the top. You can use chocolate piping to make a number of other decorations.

Scribbles

You can have lots of fun making your own freehand piped chocolate designs. Line a large baking sheet or cutting board with baking parchment. Melt the chocolate (see page 21) and spoon it into a small ready-made

piping bag. Drizzle the chocolate in small, self-contained lattice designs, such as hearts, circles and squares. Allow to set firm before carefully peeling from the paper. Store as before.

Feathering
Spread the top of a cake either with white glacé icing or melted white chocolate, then pipe straight lines of darker melted chocolate across the cake. Before the chocolate sets, draw a skewer through the lines; turn the cake around and draw the skewer in the opposite direction.

Continue until the top is completely "feathered." You can also use piped white chocolate on a bitter chocolate topping (see above). Place on a plate, line with baking parchment and chill until required.

Filigree scrolls
Line a large baking sheet or cutting board with baking parchment. Pipe a random, self-contained, mesh-like design in an oblong shape, approximately 2 x 6in (5 x 15cm). Bring the short ends of the baking parchment towards each other, chocolate

inside, and chill in this position, carefully wedged between two containers until set. Peel the paper away and use as a stunning centerpiece decoration for a gateau or dessert. Store as above.

Run-outs

Made in the same way as "scribbles," but the chocolate outline is filled with a contrasting color chocolate. This way you end up with solid shapes – good for making numbers, letters of the alphabet, flowers or animals. If you outline in a bitter chocolate, fill with white or milk chocolate. Pipe the outline of your design on a cutting board lined with baking parchment. Allow it to set completely, then pipe the contrasting melted chocolate in the gaps and tap the board gently to fill the outline completely and smooth the top. Allow to set firm before carefully peeling from the paper. Store as above.

CHOCOLATE LEAVES

The safest leaves to use for this are bay leaves, as you'll know for sure that they are not poisonous. Wash the leaves carefully and pat thoroughly dry. Melt the chocolate (see page 21). Using a small pastry brush, coat the leaves with melted chocolate. Place on a cutting board lined with baking parchment and allow to set. Peel away the leaves. Place on a plate, line with baking parchment and chill until required.

CHOCOLATE DROPS

Melt chocolate (see page 21). Drop small teaspoonfuls of the chocolate in pools onto baking trays lined with baking parchment. Tap the tray lightly on the work surface to smooth out the chocolate. Sprinkle with edible silver dragees or other similar cake decorations and allow to set in a cool place. Once set, peel from the paper. They make tempting "buttons" to decorate iced cakes and buns. Store as above.

CHOCOLATE CUT-OUTS

Melt chocolate (see page 21) and spread in a thin layer onto a tray or cutting board lined with baking parchment. Leave in a cool place until firm, but not hard (do not refrigerate). Using a sharp knife or small pastry cutters, cut out shapes to your chosen design, and carefully peel away from the paper. Store as above. These cut-outs are great for sticking into whipped cream on top of cakes, trifles, sundaes and other chilled desserts, or laid flat to decorate small iced cakes and cupcakes.

CHOCOLATE RIBBONS

Cut out strips of baking parchment about 1 x 12in (2.5 x 30cm). Line up a row of spoons on your work surface (all will become clear!). Brush each parchment strip with melted chocolate and then drape the parchment over the handles of the spoons to make waves. Leave until set, then carefully peel away the paper. Break into different lengths as desired and pile on top of cakes and desserts. Dust with cocoa powder or confectioner's sugar if liked. Store as above.

CHOCOLATE CASES

You can use chocolate in several ways to encase other ingredients or provide a container for various fillings:

Boxes

Melt chocolate (see page 21) and spread in a thin layer onto a tray or cutting board lined with baking parchment. Leave in a cool place until firm, but not hard (do not refrigerate). Using a sharp knife, cut out even sized squares, and peel away from the paper. Place on a plate, line with baking

parchment and chill until required. Use to form chocolate edges for cubes of chocolate cake, securing on the sides of the cake using jam or frosting.

Cups

Decide on the size you want to make and put either two cupcake liners or two petit four liners inside each other. Melt chocolate (see page 21), and, using a spoon or pastry brush, completely coat the bottom and inside of the liners. Allow to set, then repeat with a second layer of chocolate. Allow to set for at least 2 hours. Carefully peel away the paper case and place the chocolate cup on a flat plate. Cover lightly and keep in the fridge until required. Fill smaller cups with a piped mousse, truffle filling or flavored whipped cream. Use larger cups as a basket for fruit salad or ice cream.
NOTE: This method also works well for making your own "free-form" cups using double layers of aluminium foil.

Casing

You can make thick bands of chocolate to wrap around circular, freestanding chilled desserts to give them a stunning finish. Simply melt chocolate (see page 21) and then coat onto double-thickness strips of baking parchment. Cut the parchment to fit the size of your chosen dessert. Carefully wrap the wet chocolate strips around the dessert, chocolate-side inwards, working quickly as the chocolate will set on contact. Either chill or freeze depending on the recipe. Carefully peel away the paper, leaving the chocolate in place when ready to serve. This idea works well to give a chocolate "collar" to set mousses and iced soufflés.

DIPPING AND COATING FRUITS AND SWEETS

This is one of the simplest and most effective ways of using chocolate as a coating agent. All sorts of sweets, as well as fresh or dried fruit pieces, can be coated in chocolate. Tempered couverture chocolate (see page 17) will give the best result, but any other type of melted chocolate can be used if the dipped item is then chilled immediately. Not all fresh fruit is suitable for chocolate coating – choose either small whole fruits like cherries or kumquats, or if the fruit is cut, make sure the surface is as dry as possible, otherwise the juices from the fruit will spoil the chocolate as it is dipped.

Full coating

Use a fondue fork, skewer or specialist dipping fork to lower the sweet or piece of fruit into the chocolate. Turn to coat completely and lift out of the melted chocolate, tapping gently on the edge of the bowl to remove excess chocolate. Place on a baking parchment-lined board. If you want to set a decoration on the top or decorate with sprinkles, chopped nuts or shredded coconut, do this as soon as possible before the chocolate sets.

Half dipping

Hold the sweet or fruit between your fingers or a small pair of tongs; dip half the item in melted chocolate and place on baking parchment as above.
NOTE: If using fresh whole or cut fruit, keep the dipped fruit in the fridge until ready to serve. Best served as soon as possible before the fruit deteriorates.

COCOA STENCILS

If you're lacking inspiration for a way to finish off the top of a cake, dessert or pie, this decoration is particularly good if you don't have the time to make an icing or you want to avoid too much sweetness and yet still add good chocolate flavor. Lay a paper doily on top of the cake, dust lightly with cocoa powder and carefully remove the doily to reveal the patterned surface. You could add a sprinkling of confectioner's sugar as well, before or after the cocoa, to add highlights and a touch of sweetness. You can use any sort of paper template you want, or make your own from baking parchment.

FLAVORING AND COLORING CHOCOLATE

Ideally, additional flavorings to complement chocolate should be added to the other ingredients in your chosen recipe. If you are adding liquid flavorings to melting chocolate, they have to be added very carefully to prevent burning or causing the chocolate to thicken and become lumpy (see page 22). Drier flavorings like spices, citrus zest or vanilla bean paste can be mixed into melted chocolate, but the chocolate should then be used as quickly as possible.

White chocolate can be colored using standard food colorings, but you will need to take into account the fact that the basic color of the chocolate is not pure white. It is best to experiment with a small amount of melted chocolate and a few drops of coloring to make sure you are happy with the shade and to avoid disappointment and wastage. Colored chocolate can be used to make fillings for homemade chocolates, shells for Easter eggs or for making any of the decorations mentioned in the previous pages.

TEMPERING

This is the process of gently heating and cooling chocolate to stabilize the emulsification of cocoa solids and butterfat. It is a professional technique carried out using couverture chocolate (see page 17) and allows chocolate to shrink quickly (important for unmolding) and be stored at room temperature for longer without loss of texture, flavor or glossy appearance. The professional chocolate-maker would use a special tempering machine, but the technique can be carried out in the domestic kitchen on a small scale.

Melt the couverture chocolate (see page 17) to a temperature of about 110°F (45°C) and stir using a plastic spatula (avoid metal) until completely smooth.

Pour three-quarters of the chocolate onto a clean marble slab or board and spread across the board using the spatula. Scrape the chocolate back into a pool and then spread out again. Continue this process for about 5 minutes until the chocolate is smooth and doesn't form streaks.

Scrape this chocolate back into the bowl with the remaining quarter and mix the two batches together. The tempering process is complete and the chocolate is now ready to use.

Cakes & muffins

No tea or coffee shop dessert case would be complete without a chocolate cake of some description. Chocolate cakes are a favorite with young and old alike, and are always considered a treat.

In this chapter you'll find chocolate cakes of all different shapes and sizes, and flavors to suit all tastes. It still amazes me just how many ways there are to make a chocolate cake, and the different results each method gives. I've tried to include as many as I can.

Over the next few pages, you'll find little cupcake and muffins that the kids will love; a classic tea-time loaf cake and also a variety of larger cakes, from white to bitter and covering the whole range in between. I've included a gluten-free cake and a light, airy sponge cake that is low in fat but still has a good chocolatey flavor.

Most of the cakes are covered with frostings and icings and if you've been inspired by what you've read so far, you'll decorate them using the ideas given on pages 22–28.

Chocolate truffle cake

Decadent

I've baked this cake for several special occasions and it never fails to impress. For weddings, birthdays and Christmas, it's one of the best cakes ever.

Serves 12

15oz (450g) **70% cocoa bitter chocolate**
2 sticks **unsalted butter**
6 **large eggs,** separated
Scant 1½ cups (250g) **dark brown sugar**
6 Tbsp **dark rum or** freshly squeezed orange juice
1 tsp **vanilla extract**
1½ cups (180g) **self-rising flour**
1 cup (125g) **ground almonds**
1 **quantity Glossy chocolate cream** (see page 163)
Piped chocolate decorations (see page 24)
Few raspberries, to decorate
Light cream (optional), to serve

Preheat the oven to 350°F (180°C). Fill a roasting pan with water and place this in the bottom of the oven as it heats up. Grease and line a 10-in (25-cm) diameter, 2-in (5-cm) deep, round cake pan.

Break the chocolate into pieces and place in a heatproof bowl over a pan of gently simmering water. Cut the butter into small cubes and add to the chocolate. Allow to melt, then remove the bowl from over the water and set aside to cool for 15 minutes.

Meanwhile, in a clean bowl, whisk the egg yolks and sugar together until thick, pale and creamy. In another bowl, whisk the egg whites until stiff but not dry.

Stir the melted chocolate mixture into the whisked egg yolks and sugar. Add the rum or orange juice and vanilla extract. Sift in the flour and add the ground almonds and whisked egg whites. Carefully fold the ingredients together until well mixed, taking care not to beat too much air out of the mixture. Transfer to the prepared cake pan, smooth the top and bake in the center of the oven for 50–55 minutes or until just firm to the touch. Allow to cool in the pan on a wire rack for 30 minutes, before removing from the pan and placing back on the wire rack to cool completely.

To serve, spread the Glossy chocolate cream thickly and evenly oven the top and sides of the cake. Decorate and serve on its own or with light cream.

Chocolate truffle cake

Key lime surprise cake

Key lime surprise cake

Zesty

This recipe uses a shortcut to the typical combination of eggs and fat used in cake baking: mayonnaise. You'll be surprised at how good the results are. Make sure you choose a very plain mayo though – garlic or mustard don't taste nice with chocolate!

Serves 8

2 cups (250g) **self-rising flour**
½ cup (60g) **cocoa powder**
¼ tsp **baking powder**
1¼ cups (200g) **light brown sugar**
1 tsp **vanilla extract**
Scant 1 cup (200ml) **cold water**
Scant 1 cup (225g) **plain, good-quality mayonnaise**

For the topping:
3½oz (100g) **white chocolate**
¼ stick (30g) **unsalted butter**
1 cup (150g) **confectioner's sugar**
Finely grated **rind and juice** 1 **lime**
Strips of lime zest, to decorate

Preheat the oven to 350°F (180°C). Grease and line a 9-in (23-cm) diameter, 2-in (5-cm) deep, round cake pan. Sift the flour, cocoa and baking powder into a mixing bowl and stir in the sugar. Make a well in the center. Add the vanilla extract, water and mayonnaise, and carefully whisk the ingredients together to form a thick, smooth batter.

Transfer to the prepared cake pan and bake in the oven for 50–60 minutes or until the cake feels firm to the touch. Allow to cool in the pan on a wire rack for 30 minutes, before removing from the pan and placing back on the wire rack to cool completely.

Meanwhile, break the chocolate into a small heatproof bowl. Add the butter and place over a saucepan of gently simmering water until melted. Remove the bowl from the water and sift in the confectioner's sugar. Add the lime rind and mix together, adding sufficient lime juice to form a thick, smooth frosting. Spread over the cooled cake and sprinkle with lime zest to decorate.

Chocolate jelly roll

Classic

This familiar sponge cake takes me back to my school days when this was one of the traditional cake methods I had to perfect in order to pass my cooking exam. Sifting the flour twice and adding the hot water really makes a difference to the texture.

Serves 6–8

3 **large eggs**
½ cup (100g) **superfine sugar**
⅔ cup (90g) **all-purpose flour**
2 Tbsp + 1 tsp **cocoa powder**
1 Tbsp **hot, boiled water**
1 **quantity Chocolate buttercream (see page 162)**
Scant 1 cup (100g) **good-quality cherry conserve or jelly**
1 Tbsp **confectioner's sugar**

Preheat the oven to 425°F (220°C). Grease a 13 x 9-in (33 x 23-cm) jelly roll pan. Cut a piece of baking parchment about 2 in (5cm) larger all around than the pan. Press the parchment into the pan, creasing to fit the sides. Cut the parchment at the corners of the pan and overlap the cut paper to fit snugly.

Put the eggs and sugar in a large, clean bowl and set in a large bowl of hot water. Whisk until thick, pale and creamy – about 5 minutes. Remove from the bowl of water and continue to whisk for a further 3 minutes. You should be able to leave a trail of a spoon in the mixture when it is whisked sufficiently.

Sift the flour and 2 Tbsp cocoa first onto a sheet of wax paper and then fold it into the creamy mixture. Add the hot water and carefully fold the mixtures together using a metal spoon.

Pour the mixture into the prepared pan and tilt the pan backwards and forwards to spread the mixture in an even layer. Bake in the oven for 8–10 minutes until well risen and just firm to the touch.

Meanwhile, place a sheet of wax paper on a clean, damp tea towel. Working quickly, turn out the finished cake onto the paper and cut off the crusts. Cover with another sheet of wax paper and roll up the cake from a short side, with the paper inside. Wrap in the tea towel and allow to cool.

To serve, carefully unroll the sponge and discard the paper. Spread with the Chocolate buttercream and then the conserve or jelly, and roll up again. Dust with confectioner's sugar and remaining cocoa powder. Slice to serve.

Chocolate jelly roll

White chocolate celebration cake

White chocolate celebration cake

Rich

My sister-in-law Sarah is a great baker – much to the delight of my brother. She baked this cake for my 40th birthday and it was truly delicious. It makes a great alternative dessert.

Serves 10

4oz (125g) **white chocolate**
3 **large egg whites**
Scant 2 cups (225g) **self-rising flour**
Scant 1 cup (180g) **superfine sugar**
1 Tbsp **baking powder**
¾ cup (180ml) **whole milk**
¾ tsp **vanilla extract**
¾ stick (90g) **unsalted butter**, melted
1 **quantity Glossy white chocolate cream (see page 163)**
Cocoa stencils (see page 28), to decorate

Preheat the oven to 350°F (180°C). Grease and line a deep 8-in (20-cm) cake pan. Break the chocolate into pieces and place in a heatproof bowl over a pan of gently simmering water. Allow to melt, then remove from the water and set aside.

Meanwhile, in a large grease-free bowl, whisk the egg whites until stiff but not dry and set aside. Sift the flour, sugar and baking powder into another bowl. Make a well in the center and pour in the milk and add the vanilla extract and melted butter. Whisk gently to form a thick batter, then stir in the melted chocolate. Finally fold in the egg whites and pour into the prepared pan. Smooth the top and bake in the oven for about 50 minutes until golden, risen and firm to the touch. Allow to cool in the pan on a wire rack for 10 minutes, before removing from the pan and placing back onto the wire rack to cool completely.

When the cake is cool, slice the cake horizontally in two and spread half of the Glossy white chocolate cream thickly over one half of the cake. Sandwich the cake together and spread the remaining cream thickly over the top. Decorate with a cocoa stencil before serving.

Chocolate orange polenta cake

Contemporary

It can be quite difficult baking something that's indulgent and decadent if you're on a gluten-free or dairy-free diet, but this cake should make the grade. It's lovely to serve as a rich dessert.

Serves 8

¾ cup (180ml) **sunflower oil**
Scant 1¼ cups (180g) **light brown sugar**
2 **large eggs**
2 Tbsp **cocoa powder**
1 cup (150g) **ground almonds**
Finely grated **zest and juice of 1 medium orange**
Scant ¼ cup (90g) **finely ground cornmeal**
½ tsp **baking powder**
¼ quantity **Chocolate sugar syrup (see page 158)**
Fresh orange segments
Greek yogurt or soy cream, to serve

Preheat the oven to 350°F (180°C). Grease and line the base and sides of a 7-in (18-cm) round springform cake pan using baking parchment.

Whisk together the sunflower oil with the sugar and eggs. Sift in the cocoa powder and add the ground almonds, orange zest, cornmeal and baking powder. Mix together well and pour into the prepared pan and bake for 50–55 minutes until firm to the touch and a skewer inserted into the center comes out clean.

While the cake is baking, prepare the Chocolate sugar syrup. Stir the orange juice into the warm syrup, then set aside.

Once the cake comes out of the oven, skewer all over with a toothpick and pour the syrup over the warm cake. Cool in the pan on a wire rack, then release from the pan. To serve, arrange the orange segments on top of the cake, with Greek yogurt or soy cream on the side.

Four-layer chocolate chiffon cake

Family favorite

This uniquely American baking sensation is made with oil instead of butter, which gives the sponge a silky-soft texture – hence the name.

Serves 12

3oz (90g) **70% cocoa bitter chocolate**

2 cups (250g) **self-rising flour**

1 Tbsp **baking powder**

Scant 1½ cups (300g) **superfine sugar**

6 **eggs, separated**

½ cup (100ml) **corn oil**

½ cup (100ml) **cold water**

½ tsp **cream of tartar**

2 **quantities of Glossy milk chocolate cream (see page 163)**

1oz (30g) **70% cocoa bitter chocolate**, melted (see page 21), for piping

Preheat the oven to 350°F (180°C). Grease and line two 9-in (23-cm) round springform cake pans with baking parchment. Break the chocolate into pieces and place in a small heatproof bowl over a pan of gently simmering water. Allow to melt, then remove from the water and set aside for 5 minutes.

Meanwhile, sift the flour and baking powder into a bowl and stir in the sugar. In a separate bowl, mix together the egg yolks, oil and water. In a third bowl, whisk the egg whites with the cream of tartar until stiff.

Make a well in the flour and baking powder and pour the egg and oil mixture into the well and add the warm chocolate. Mix together to form a smooth batter. Carefully fold the egg whites into the chocolate batter until thoroughly mixed. Divide between the two cake pans and bake for about 35 minutes until risen and firm to the touch. Cool for 10 minutes in the pans and then turn onto wire racks to cool completely.

When the cake has cooled, carefully cut each cake horizontally in half. Spread half of the Glossy milk chocolate cream over three of the layers. Sandwich the layers together in a neat stack and top with the fourth cake layer. Spread the remaining chocolate cream over the top and sides of the cake. Pipe the melted bitter chocolate over the top of the cake to decorate – for example, pipe the word "chocolate" repeatedly over the surface.

Old-fashioned marbled loaf cake

Old-fashioned marbled loaf cake

Traditional

I love a "proper" cakey cake – uniced, with a dense, crumbly texture that is ideally accompanied by a cup of tea or coffee. If you want to jazz it up a bit, drizzle with some Chocolate glacé icing (see page 163).

Serves 8

1½oz (45g) **semisweet chocolate**
2 tsp **hot, boiled water**
½ tsp **vanilla extract**
1½ sticks (180g) **unsalted butter, softened**
Scant 1 cup (180g) **superfine sugar**
3 **large eggs,** beaten
2 cups (250g) **all-purpose flour**
1½ tsp **baking powder**
Generous ¼ cup (45g) **ground almonds**
1½ Tbsp **milk**

Preheat the oven to 350°F (180°C). Grease and line a 2-lb (1-kg) loaf pan with baking parchment Break the chocolate into pieces and place in a small heatproof bowl over a pan of gently simmering water. Allow to melt, then remove from the water and set aside to cool for 15 minutes. Stir in the water and the vanilla extract.

Put the butter and sugar in a separate bowl and beat together until pale and fluffy. Beat in the eggs one at a time. Sift in the flour and baking powder and add the ground almonds and milk. Gently fold the dry ingredients into the creamed mixture. Spoon half the mixture into another bowl and mix in the melted chocolate.

Drop alternate spoonfuls of the two mixtures into the prepared pan, gently swirling the two together to give a marbled effect. The mixture should be of dropping consistency, so thin with a little more milk if the mixture is too thick. Smooth the top and bake in the oven for about 45 minutes until risen, firm to the touch and a skewer inserted into the center comes out clean. Cool in the pan for 15 minutes, then turn onto a wire rack to cool completely.

Wrap the cooled cake well and store for 24 hours before slicing thickly to serve.

Chocolate angel cake

Feather-light

This is one of the best fat-free sponge cakes I've ever made. It rises well and has a soft, aerated texture. The contrasting white frosting is the perfect disguise for a light chocolate sponge interior.

Serves 8–10

1 cup (100g) **all-purpose flour**
Scant 1 cup (2 Tbsp) **cocoa powder**
Scant 1 cup (180g) **superfine sugar**
Pinch **of salt**
7 **large egg whites**
1 level tsp **cream of tartar**
1 tsp **vanilla extract**
1 **quantity of White vanilla frosting
   (see page 161)**
Edible silver dragees, to decorate

Preheat the oven to 350°F (180°C). Grease and line a deep 8-in (20-cm) diameter round cake pan with baking parchment. Sift the flour and cocoa powder with 7 Tbsp of the superfine sugar and the salt in a bowl. Set aside.

Place the egg whites in a large grease-free bowl and whisk until foamy but not stiff. Add the cream of tartar and 2 Tbsp of the remaining superfine sugar. Whisk until the egg whites form soft peaks. Add the vanilla extract and remaining sugar, and fold in using a large metal spoon. Gently sift in the flour, cocoa and sugar mixture, folding it in as you go.

Transfer the mixture to the prepared pan and smooth the top. Bake in the center of the oven for 30–35 minutes until firm to the touch and a skewer inserted into the center comes out clean. Leave to cool in the pan for 15 minutes, then remove from the pan and transfer to a wire rack to cool completely.

Peel away the parchment and slice the cake horizontally in half. Spread one-third of the White vanilla frosting over one cake half and sandwich the other half on top. Transfer to a serving plate, cover with the remaining frosting and leave for 30 minutes to set before serving decorated with silver dragees.

Chocolate angel cake

Devil's food cake

Devil's food cake

Wicked

I've eaten many versions of this well-known cake – some with fresh chocolate cream and others, like this one, with a thick butter frosting. What every recipe has in common though is that they're all very chocolatey!

Serves 10

4oz (125g) **70% cocoa bitter chocolate**
2 cups (250g) **self-rising flour**
1¼ cups (275g) **superfine sugar**
1¼ cups (300ml) **buttermilk**
1 stick (125g) **unsalted butter, softened**
3 **eggs,** beaten
1½ tsp **baking soda**
½ tsp **baking powder**
1 tsp **vanilla extract**
1 **quantity Bitter chocolate fudge frosting (see page 162)**
Bitter chocolate curls (see page 23), to decorate

Preheat the oven to 350ºF (180ºC). Grease and line two 9-in (23-cm) round springform cake pans with baking parchment. Break the chocolate into pieces and place in a small heatproof bowl over a pan of gently simmering water. Allow to melt, then remove from the water and set aside to cool for 5 minutes.

Put all the remaining ingredients, except the frosting and chocolate curls, in a large bowl, and add the warm melted chocolate. Mix all the ingredients together well and then beat for 2 minutes until smooth and creamy.

Divide the mixture between the pans and smooth over the tops. Bake for 35–40 minutes until risen and firm to the touch. Cool in the pans for 10 minutes and then turn onto wire racks to cool completely.

To serve, sandwich the two cake halves together with one-third of the Bitter chocolate fudge frosting and spread the remaining frosting over the sides and top of the cake. Serve piled high with Chocolate curls.

Pineapple chocolate muffins

Moist

Adding crushed pineapple to a mixture will make it dense and moist. The flavor and texture improves with time, so store, uniced, for at least 24 hours before serving.

Makes 10

Scant 2 cups (225g) **all-purpose flour**
2 Tbsp **cocoa powder**
1 tsp **baking powder**
1 tsp **baking soda**
¼ tsp **salt**
Scant 1¼ cups (180g) **dark brown sugar**
1½ sticks (180g) **unsalted butter**
2 **eggs**, beaten
½ cup (100ml) **whole milk**
1 cup (250g) **crushed canned pineapple**, drained
1¼ cups (180g) **confectioner's sugar**
½ cup (30g) **unsweetened desiccated coconut**
Dried pineapple slices, to decorate

Preheat the oven to 350°F (180°C). Line 10 cups of a deep 12-bun muffin pan with paper muffin liners. Sift the flour, cocoa, baking powder, baking soda and salt into a mixing bowl. Stir in the sugar and make a well in the center.

Melt half the butter and pour into the well along with the eggs and milk to form a thick batter. Fold in the crushed pineapple.

Divide the mixture equally among the cupcake liners and bake in the oven for about 30 minutes until risen and lightly golden. Transfer to a wire rack to cool completely. Wrap well and store for 24 hours before serving.

To serve, beat the remaining butter until soft and gradually sift in the confectioner's sugar, beating well, and add the coconut to form a fluffy icing. Spread thickly over each muffin before serving and top each muffin with a slice of dried pineapple.

Pineapple chocolate muffins

Cappuccino muffins

Mocha

Coffee is one of my favorite flavors and these muffins have a good proportion of coffee and chocolate. You could make mini versions to serve as petit fours.

Makes 12

½ cup (60g) **semisweet-chocolate covered coffee beans**
3 cups (350g) **self-rising flour**
1 cup (125g) **light brown sugar**
Generous 1 cup (200g) **semisweet chocolate chips**
2 **eggs**, beaten
1 stick (125g) **butter,** melted
Scant 1 cup (200ml) **whole milk**
1 Tbsp **confectioner's sugar**
1 tsp **hot chocolate mix**

Preheat the oven to 375°F (190°C). Line a 12-bun muffin pan with 12 paper liners. Grind the chocolate coffee beans in a coffee grinder or blender until fine and well ground.

Sift the flour into a bowl and fold in the ground coffee beans, sugar and chocolate chips. Make a well in the center.

Mix the eggs, melted butter and milk together and pour into the well. Mix to form a smooth batter, taking care not to overmix. Divide the batter equally between the paper liners and bake for about 30 minutes until risen and firm to the touch. Transfer to a wire rack to cool.

Serve warm, dusted lightly with confectioner's sugar and then a little hot chocolate mix.

White chocolate and lemon muffins

Zesty

This is a reduced-fat recipe that produces a surprisingly light muffin. They will keep for a couple of days in an airtight container but are best served warm.

Makes 8

2 cups (250g) **self-rising flour**
½ tsp **baking powder**
¼ cup (60g) **superfine sugar**
4oz (125g) **white chocolate,**
    cut into small chunks
2 **large eggs,** separated
Finely grated **rind and juice of**
    1 **small lemon**
6 Tbsp **low-fat natural yogurt**
4 Tbsp **corn oil**
4 Tbsp **water**
Warmed **lemon curd or lemon jelly**
    (optional), to serve

Preheat the oven to 400°F (200°C). Line 8 cups of a muffin pan with paper muffin liners. Sift the flour and baking powder into a bowl and stir in the sugar and chocolate chunks. Make a well in the center.

Mix together the egg yolks, lemon rind and juice, yogurt, oil and water. Whisk the egg whites in a grease-free bowl until stiff but not too dry. Pour the lemon and yogurt mixture into the well and mix to form a dropping consistency, taking care not to overmix. Gently fold in the egg whites and divide the mixture equally between the muffin liners.

Bake in the oven for about 25 minutes until well risen and golden brown. Transfer to a wire rack to cool. Serve warm with lemon curd or lemon jelly to spoon over if desired.

Chocolate blueberry cupcakes

Chocolate blueberry cupcakes

Kids' favorite

These sweet little cakes make an ideal treat at a children's party.
A lilac-colored icing gives a pretty finishing touch, but a chocolate one is just
as good.

Makes 16

½ cup (60g) **cocoa powder**
Scant 1 cup (200ml) **warm, boiled**
  water
1 stick (125g) **butter, softened**
Scant 2 cups (300g) **light brown sugar**
2 **eggs,** beaten
1½ cups (180g) **self-rising flour**
⅔ cup (200g) **blueberries,** thawed
  if frozen
1¼ cups (200g) **confectioner's sugar**
5–6 tsp **unsweetened blueberry**
  juice drink
Crystallized violets, to decorate

Preheat the oven to 375°F (190°C). Put
16 paper cupcake liners into a muffin
pan. Sift the cocoa into a small bowl
and whisk in the water.

In another bowl, beat the butter and
sugar together until pale and creamy,
and gradually beat in the eggs and
cocoa mixture. Sift in the flour and fold
the ingredients together, along with the
blueberries.

Divide the mixture equally between the
cupcake liners and bake in the oven
for about 20 minutes until risen to the
tops of the liners and just firm to the
touch. Transfer to a wire rack to cool.

For the icing, sift the confectioner's
sugar into a bowl and bind together
with sufficient blueberry juice to form a
smooth, spreadable icing. Spread
neatly over each cupcake and
decorate with crystallized violets. Allow
the icing to set for a few minutes
before serving.

Chocolate chunk and raspberry muffins

Fruity

Chocolate and raspberry go so well together, the sweetness of the chocolate cutting through the tartness of the raspberry. These muffins are a real treat.

Makes 10

2 cups (250g) **self-rising flour**
Generous ½ cup (125g) **unbleached superfine sugar**
Generous ½ cup (125g) **milk chocolate chunks**
2 **eggs,** beaten
⅔ cup (150ml) **whole milk**
1 stick (125g) **butter,** melted
⅔ cup (200g) **fresh raspberries**
1 **quantity Chocolate glacé icing** (see page 163, optional)

Preheat the oven to 375°F (190°C). Put 10 paper muffin liners into a deep muffin pan.

Sift the flour into a bowl and gently stir in the sugar and chocolate chunks and make a well in the center. Mix the eggs, milk and melted butter together and pour into the well, stirring to form a stiff batter, but taking care not to overmix. Carefully fold in the raspberries.

Divide the batter equally among the muffin liners. Smooth the tops slightly and bake in the oven for 35–40 minutes, until risen and lightly golden. Transfer to a wire rack to cool.

Best served warm on day of baking. If liked, top with Chocolate glacé icing.

Chocolate chunk and raspberry muffins

Toffee chocolate cupcakes

Tea-time treat

My favorite chocolates are those with caramel, fudge or toffee centers, and with this in mind, I developed this recipe. I'm sure it will be popular with children and adults alike.

Makes 14

1⅔ cups (200g) **self-rising flour**
½ cup (100g) **unbleached superfine sugar**
2 Tbsp **cocoa powder**
½ Tsp **baking powder**
Generous ¼ cup (75ml) **sunflower oil**
⅔ cup (75ml) **buttermilk**
2 **eggs**, beaten
1 Tbsp **corn syrup**
½ cup (100g) **toffee- or caramel-flavored spread**
2oz (60g) **milk chocolate**

Preheat the oven to 325°F (160°C). Put 14 paper cupcake liners into a cupcake pan. Sift the flour, sugar, cocoa and baking powder into a bowl and make a well in the center.

Whisk together the oil, buttermilk, eggs and syrup and pour into the well. Mix together to form a smooth batter, taking care not to overmix. Divide the mixture equally among the cupcake liners and bake in the oven for about 20 minutes until risen and firm to the touch. Transfer to a wire rack to cool.

Slice off the top of each cupcake and spread with toffee spread. Replace the tops. Break the chocolate into a small heatproof bowl and place over a saucepan of gently simmering water until melted. Drizzle the chocolate over the top of each cupcake. Allow to set for a few minutes before serving.

Toffee chocolate cupcakes

Pies, tarts & pastries

After cake-baking, pastry-making is next on my list of favorites. I prefer the flavor and texture of homemade pastry – it's usually more crumbly, buttery and flavorsome. But it does take time and a bit of skill, and if you don't have the confidence, then there are some good ready-made pastry doughs and pie shells available. Choose a good-quality brand so that the flavor of the pastry doesn't detract from the filling or topping that you're making to go with it.

When I was researching recipes for this chapter, I soon discovered that there aren't that many classic chocolate pies. What you'll find over the next few pages are a collection of favorites with a chocolate addition, such as the nutty and sweet Chocolate pecan pie, some classic pastries like the French breakfast-time treat Mini pain au chocolat, alongside some new ideas – Chocolate date strudel with crisp, buttery flakes of pastry, and a creamy White chocolate and berry pie.

Although pies are usually made from short pastry, I've included recipes using filo, choux and puff pastry as well as pie shells made using cookie crumbs. I hope you enjoy them as much I as did!

Chocolate and cherry puffs

Melt-in-your-mouth

These pastries are very straightforward to assemble and can be prepared in advance, so you can simply bake them just before serving. Serve while the chocolate is still molten.

Makes 8

1lb (500g) **ready-made puff pastry,** thawed if frozen
6oz (180g) **semisweet chocolate**
8 Tbsp **cherry pie filling**
1 **egg,** beaten

Preheat the oven to 400°F (200°C). On a lightly-floured surface, roll out the pastry to approximately a 16-in (40-cm) square. Cut out sixteen 4-in (10-cm) diameter circles using a pastry cutter.

Arrange eight circles on a large baking sheet lined with baking parchment. Divide the chocolate into eight pieces and place chocolate in the center of each circle. Top each piece of pastry with 1 Tbsp cherry pie filling. Brush the edges with beaten egg and cover with the remaining pastry circles. Seal the edges well.

Slash the tops lightly with a sharp knife and brush with beaten egg. Bake for 20–25 minutes until puffed up and golden. Best served warm.

Rich chocolate and apricot tart

Dark

If your taste in chocolate is towards the bitter end of the scale, then this tart is for you. You can make it with semisweet or an unsweetened, lesser cocoa percentage chocolate if you prefer.

Serves 8

1 quantity Chocolate pastry (see page 161) or 1 ready-made 9-in (23-cm) chocolate pie crust
6 Tbsp **good quality apricot conserve or jelly,** softened
1 stick (125g) **unsalted butter**
5oz (150g) **unsweetened or 85% (or above) cocoa bitter chocolate,** broken into pieces
3 **eggs**
Scant ½ cup (3oz) **superfine sugar**
Cocoa powder and confectioner's sugar, to dust
Crème fraîche, to serve

Preheat the oven to 400°F (200°C). Make and bake the Chocolate pastry crust. Reduce the oven temperature to 350°F (180°C).

Spread the apricot conserve in a thin layer over the base of the pastry crust. Put the butter and chocolate in a heatproof bowl over a saucepan of gently simmering water until melted. Remove from the water and set aside. Meanwhile, whisk the eggs and sugar together until pale and creamy.

Gently fold the melted chocolate and butter into the egg mixture until evenly incorporated and spoon over the pastry. Smooth the surface and bake for about 25 minutes until the top has formed a crust. Let stand for 10 minutes before removing from the pan if you plan to serve it hot, otherwise allow to cool in the pan and then chill for at least 1 hour before serving. Serve hot or cold, dusted with cocoa and confectioner's sugar, accompanied by crème fraîche.

Mini pain au chocolat

Mini pain au chocolat

Flaky

This is perfect mid-morning with a cup of coffee. Half pastry, half bread – it's deliciously flaky with a soft chocolate center.

Makes 12

2¼ cups (275g) **all-purpose flour**
1 Tbsp **superfine sugar**
½ tsp **salt**
2 Tbsp (30g) **lard or white vegetable fat**
1 tsp **fast-acting dried yeast**
⅔ cup (150ml) **whole milk, slightly warm**
¾ stick (90g) **unsalted butter**
1 **egg,** beaten
12 **small pieces** (approx. 2oz/60g) **semisweet chocolate**
¼ cup (30g) **confectioner's sugar**

Sift the flour into a mixing bowl and stir in the sugar and salt. Rub in the fat to form fine breadcrumbs. Stir in the yeast.

Make a well in the center and pour in most of the milk. Mix with your fingers, then tip on to a lightly-floured work surface. Bring together and knead lightly until you have a dough slightly softer than a pastry mixture; add more milk if necessary. Lightly flour the bowl and place the dough back in it. Cover loosely and set in a warm place for about an hour until doubled in size.

Gently reknead the dough to form a smooth ball. Roll the dough out to form an oblong 15 x 6in (38 x 15cm) and place the stick of butter in the center. Fold the dough over the butter, top and bottom, to cover it and press the edges to seal. Roll the dough out gently to form an oblong the same size as before. Fold the top third down and the bottom third up, and turn 90 degrees. Cover and rest for 10 minutes. Repeat the rolling, folding and turning twice more. Transfer to a floured plate, cover and chill for 30 minutes.

Roll out to 12 x 8in (30 x 20cm). Cut in two lengthways and then cut each piece into six oblongs to give 12 pieces. Brush each with beaten egg and then place a piece of chocolate in the center. On each piece fold the bottom third up and the top third down. Turn over and press down to seal the edges to enclose the chocolate.

Transfer to a large baking sheet and cover loosely with greased clear food wrap. Set in a warm place for about 30 minutes until slightly risen. Preheat the oven to 425°F (220°C).

Brush with beaten egg and bake for about 15 minutes until puffed up and golden. Transfer to a wire rack to cool. Best served warm, dusted with confectioner's sugar.

Tiramisu chocolate choux buns

Italian-style

Choux is a light puffy pastry that makes the perfect casing for a creamy coffee filling. Whipped cream or custard are also popular fillings. Always fill just before serving to enjoy the pastry crisp.

Serves 8

For the choux pastry:
1¼ cups (150g) **all-purpose flour**
2 Tbsp **cocoa powder**
½ tsp **salt**
1 Tbsp **superfine sugar**
1 cup (250ml) **cold water**
1 stick (125g) **unsalted butter,**
   cut into pieces
Approx. 4 **eggs,** beaten

For the filling:
⅔ cup (150ml) **whipping cream**
2 Tbsp **confectioner's sugar**
⅔ cup (150g) **mascarpone cheese**
1 tsp **instant coffee granules,**
   dissolved in 2 tsp cooled boiled
   water
1 Tbsp **brandy (optional)**

To serve:
1 **quantity Chocolate glacé icing**
   (see page 163)
Cocoa powder, to dust

Preheat the oven to 425°F (220°C). Lightly grease a large baking sheet. Sift the flour, cocoa, salt and sugar onto a sheet of wax paper. Put the water in a saucepan with the butter and bring to a boil.

Remove from the heat. Bend the wax paper into a chute shape; this makes it easier to add the sifted ingredients immediately and all at once. Beat vigorously until the mixture forms a smooth ball in the saucepan. Cool for 10 minutes, then gradually beat in sufficient egg to form a thick, shiny mixture that gently drops off the spoon.

Sprinkle the baking sheet lightly with water and then drop eight mounds approximately 3in (7.5cm) in diameter, at least 2in (5cm) apart on the baking sheet. Bake for about 40 minutes until puffed up and firm. Using a serrated knife, slice one-quarter of the way around the side of each bun to allow the steam to escape. Arrange on a wire rack to cool completely.

For the filling, whip the cream until just peaking. Sift in the confectioner's sugar and add the mascarpone cheese, coffee and brandy, if using, and continue whisking until firm enough to spoon. Cover and chill until required.

When ready to serve, spoon the coffee cream filling into the center of each bun and carefully spread with Chocolate glacé icing. Serve dusted with cocoa powder.

Chocolate pecan pie

Nutty

A classic favorite with a chocolate twist. It's a great way to enjoy the sweet earthiness of pecan nuts.

Serves 8

1 quantity Chocolate pastry (see page 161) or 10oz (300g) ready-made sweet basic pie dough
3oz (90g) semisweet chocolate
¼ stick (30g) unsalted butter
¼ cup (60g) superfine sugar
1½ tsp cornstarch
Pinch salt
⅔ cup (150ml) maple syrup
2 eggs, beaten
Scant 2 cups (200g) pecan nuts
Vanilla ice cream, to serve

Preheat the oven to 350°F (180°C). Make the Chocolate pastry and roll out and line a 9 in (23-cm) loose-bottomed flan pan. Chill until required.

Break the chocolate into pieces and place in a small heatproof bowl. Add the butter and set the bowl over a pan of gently simmering water. Allow to melt, then remove from the water and set aside to cool for 15 minutes.

Meanwhile, make the filling. In a bowl, whisk together the remaining ingredients, except the pecan nuts, and then whisk in the melted chocolate and butter. Transfer to a batter bowl.

Arrange the pecan nuts neatly in the pastry shell and set on a baking sheet. Pour over the filling and bake in the oven for about 50 minutes until set. Allow to cool in the pan, then transfer to a serving plate. Best served with vanilla ice cream.

Chocolate almond and pear tart

Juicy

Chocolate and pears go together as well as strawberries and cream. This tart is just as good hot or cold – I prefer it just warm so that the almond flavor comes through.

Serves 6–8

- 1 **quantity Chocolate pastry (see page 161) or** 10oz (300g) **ready-made sweet basic pie dough**
- 1 stick (125g) **unsalted butter, softened**
- Generous ½ cup (125g) **superfine sugar**
- 2 **eggs**
- 1 cup (125g) **ground almonds**
- 2 Tbsp **cocoa powder**
- ½ tsp **almond extract**
- 14-oz (410-g) **can pear halves in natural juice,** drained
- ⅛ cup (15g) **sliced almonds**
- 1 Tbsp **confectioner's sugar, to dust**
- **Light cream, to serve**

Preheat the oven to 375°F (190°C). Make the Chocolate pastry and roll out and line a 9-in (23-cm) loose-bottomed flan pan. Chill until required.

In a mixing bowl, cream together the butter and sugar until pale and creamy. Gradually beat in the eggs and ground almonds. Sift in the cocoa powder and fold in along with the almond extract. Spoon the mixture into the pastry shell and smooth the top.

Cut the pear halves in half and pat dry with paper towel. Gently press the pear slices into the almond filling. Sprinkle with sliced almonds and bake in the oven for 35–40 minutes until the almonds are lightly golden and the sponge is firm to the touch. Let stand for 10 minutes before removing from the pan. Dust with confectioner's sugar and serve hot or cold with light cream.

Chocolate almond and pear tart

Chocolate banoffee pie

Chocolate banoffee pie

Sweet-toothed

This pie's name comes from the combination of banana and toffee in the filling. I've added some chocolate into the mix and piled it high with whipped cream, making it an even more indulgent dessert.

Serves 6

¾ stick (90g) **butter**
1½ cups (250g) **double chocolate chip cookies,** crushed
3 **ripe medium-sized bananas**
14-oz (397-g) **can condensed milk**
1 Tbsp **cocoa powder**
1¼ cups (300ml) **heavy cream**
Grated milk chocolate, to decorate

Grease the bases and sides of six individual 3-in (8-cm) loose-bottomed cake pans or cake rings. Melt the butter in a saucepan, then remove from the heat. Mix the crushed cookies with the melted butter and divide among the six pans. Press firmly into the base of each. Slice the bananas thinly and arrange over the cookie base. Cover and chill until required.

Pour the condensed milk into a saucepan, bring to a boil and simmer over a medium heat, stirring, until the milk turns a toffee color. Remove from the heat, sift over the cocoa and add 6 Tbsp heavy cream and mix well. Spoon the toffee filling over the bananas and cookie base. Cover and chill for 30 minutes.

When ready to serve, remove the pies from the pans and place on serving plates. Whip the remaining heavy cream and pile on top of each one. Sprinkle with grated chocolate and serve.

■ *Try not to brown the condensed milk too much, otherwise the filling will set too hard.*

Chocolate date strudel

Buttery

Fresh dates have a sticky, sweet texture that makes them a perfect filling for a pastry. Combined with chocolate, nuts and cinnamon, this pastry creation makes a delicious feast on a winter's day.

Serves 8

¾ cup (60g) **chocolate cake crumbs (see page 130)**
⅓ cup (30g) **sliced almonds**, toasted
1½ cups (250g) **fresh dates**, pitted and finely chopped
¾ cup (125g) **semisweet chocolate chips**
1 tsp **ground cinnamon**
½ tsp finely grated **orange rind**
2 Tbsp freshly-squeezed **orange juice**
8 large **sheets filo pastry**
¾ stick (90g) **unsalted butter**, melted
2 Tbsp **confectioner's sugar**
1 tsp **cocoa powder**
Light cream, to serve

Preheat the oven to 400°F (200°C). Line a large baking sheet with baking parchment. In a bowl, mix together the cake crumbs, almonds, dates, chocolate chips, cinnamon, orange rind and juice and mix well.

Lay four sheets of filo pastry on the work surface, overlapping as necessary, to form a rectangle approximately 20½ x 14in (52 x 36cm). Brush well with melted butter to secure together. Layer the remaining pastry on top in the same way, brushing all over with butter.

Spread the date mixture evenly down the center of the pastry to within 1in (2.5cm) of either end. Fold the top and bottom pastry edge on top of the filling, buttering to seal. Fold the pastry over from the long sides to completely cover the filling, and brush with butter to seal. Transfer to the prepared baking sheet and brush with the remaining butter.

Bake in the oven for about 40 minutes until crisp and golden. Serve hot, dusted with confectioner's sugar and cocoa. Accompany with light cream.

Chocolate molasses tart

Old-fashioned

A variation on a favorite recipe from my school days. A real comforting pudding, but it is also lovely cold, drizzled with orange glacé icing.

Serves 6–8

¾ cup (60g) **chocolate cake crumbs** (see page 130)
1 **quantity Chocolate pastry (see page 161) or** 10oz (300g) **readymade sweet pastry**
Scant 1 cup (200g) **corn syrup**
2 Tbsp (30g) **molasses**
¼ stick (30g) **unsalted butter**
2oz (60g) **70% cocoa semisweet chocolate,** broken into pieces
½ tsp finely grated **orange rind**
2 Tbsp freshly squeezed **orange juice**
1⅔ cups (90g) **fresh white breadcrumbs**

Preheat the oven to 400°F (200°C). Roll out three-quarters of the pastry on a lightly floured surface and use to line a 8-in (20-cm) loose-bottomed flan pan. Cover and chill while making the filling.

Put the syrup, molasses, butter and chocolate in a saucepan and heat gently until melted. Remove from the heat and set aside to cool but do not allow to set, then stir in the orange rind and juice.

Sprinkle the breadcrumbs evenly over the base of the pastry shell, then slowly pour over the melted chocolate syrup. Roll out the remaining pastry thinly into an oblong 8-in (20-cm) long and cut several thin strips, re-rolling the pastry as necessary. Brush the edge of the tart with water and stick the strips to the pastry shell, forming a lattice pattern over the chocolate breadcrumbs.

Transfer to a baking tray and bake for 25–30 minutes until the filling has set and the pastry is firm. Let stand for 10 minutes before removing from the pan. Best served warm with light cream or custard.

White chocolate and berry pie

Creamy

The very rich and indulgent white chocolate in this pie is perfectly accompanied by the sharp-sweet flavor of summer berries and currants. Orange segments also make a good accompaniment.

Serves 8–10

1¼ sticks (150g) **butter**
8oz (250g) **shortbread fingers,**
    crushed
8oz (250g) **white chocolate**
1¼ cups (300ml) **sour cream**
2 Tbsp **dark rum (optional)**
1¼ cups (300ml) **heavy cream**
1 cup (250g) **prepared, assorted**
    summer berries
White chocolate decorations,
    to finish

Grease and line the base and sides of a 8-in (20-cm) springform cake pan. Melt ¾ stick (90g) butter in a saucepan, remove from the heat and then mix in the crushed shortbread. Press into the base of the pan. Chill until required.

Break the chocolate into pieces and place in a small heatproof bowl. Add the remaining butter and set the bowl over a pan of gently simmering water. Allow to melt, then remove from the water and stir in the sour cream and rum if using.

Whip the heavy cream to form soft peaks and fold into the chocolate cream. Spoon over the cookie base and smooth the top. Chill for at least 6 hours or overnight.

When ready to serve, remove from the pan and place on a serving plate. Top with the berries and finish off with white chocolate decorations of your choice (see pages 22–28 for ideas). Cut into slices to serve.

■ *This dessert will also work with milk or bittersweet chocolate.*

White chocolate and berry pie

Chocolate custard tarts

Chocolate custard tarts

Comforting

These little custard tarts make a perfect treat with coffee or tea. If you're short on time, use 10oz (300g) ready-made basic pie dough instead of making your own.

Makes 12

1 quantity Chocolate pastry (see page 161) or 10oz (300g) ready-made basic pie dough
1 egg yolk
2 Tbsp superfine sugar
1 Tbsp vanilla sugar (see tip below)
1 Tbsp all-purpose flour
1 cup (250ml) whole milk
1 Tbsp cornstarch
1oz (30g) unsweetened or 85% (or above) cocoa bitter chocolate, grated

Preheat the oven to 400°F (200°C). Make the Chocolate pastry and roll out thinly on a lightly-floured surface. Using a 3-in (7.5-cm) diameter round pastry cutter, cut out 12 circles, re-rolling the pastry as necessary, and press into tartlet pans. Lightly prick the bases and bake in the oven for about 15–20 minutes until set and firm. Set aside.

In a heatproof bowl, whisk the egg yolk and sugars together until pale, thick and creamy. Whisk in the flour with 1 Tbsp milk, then add the cornstarch and a further 1 Tbsp milk to make a smooth paste. Pour the remaining milk into a saucepan and add the grated chocolate. Heat gently, stirring, until the chocolate melts, then bring to just below boiling point and then pour over the egg and flour paste, whisking until smooth and well combined. Transfer to a saucepan and stir over a low heat until it comes to a boil and then cook for a further 2 minutes until thick, smooth and glossy.

Remove from the heat and spoon some into each pastry shell. Smooth the tops, cover the surface with buttered wax paper and leave to cool completely. Chill until ready to serve.

■ *To make vanilla sugar, simply add a couple of vanilla pods to a jar of sugar. Within a day or so the sugar will have become infused with the scent of vanilla.*

Brownies, cookies & bars

This chapter contains two of my all-time personal favorites, so it is probably the section I enjoyed writing and trying out the most. There are so many chocolate baked goods to choose from, it was difficult to narrow the selection down. But I'm sure you'll like the next few recipes as much as I do.

No chocolate book would be complete without brownies and you'll find two different recipes, as well as a white chocolate version to try. Cookies are also chocolate classics and I've included two recipes – Double chocolate and Cookie sandwiches – both are very moreish and delicious. You'll find a healthier-style bar cookie of cereal, dried fruit and chocolate chips, and two recipes for chocolate breads – one French and one Italian.

Wondering what my two personal favorites are? Crisp, sugary meringues are the first, and here I've given them a chocolate twist, and Millionaire's shortbread – the combination of buttery shortbread, thick caramel and lots of chocolate is very hard to beat!

Flourless mint chocolate brownies

Fudgey

These brownies are the perfect treat for anyone on a gluten-free diet. The texture is dense, truffley and very chocolatey, and the peppermint cream topping makes them even more yummy!

Makes 16

8oz (250g) **70% cocoa bitter chocolate**

2 sticks (250g) **unsalted butter, cut into small pieces**

1¼ cups (200g) **light brown sugar**

4 **eggs, beaten**

1 cup (150g) **ground almonds**

1½ tsp **baking powder**

Generous ¼ cup (60g) **milk chocolate chunks**

7½oz (225g) **chocolate-coated peppermint cream wafers**

Preheat the oven to 325°F (160°C). Grease and line with baking parchment a deep 9-in (23-cm) square cake pan. Break the chocolate into pieces and place in a heatproof bowl. Add the butter and set the bowl over a pan of gently simmering water. Allow to melt, then remove from the water and stir in the sugar. Set aside to cool for 10 minutes.

Gradually whisk the eggs into the chocolate to make a thick, glossy mixture. Add the ground almonds, baking powder and chocolate chunks, and carefully fold in until well combined.

Transfer to the prepared pan and smooth over the top. Bake in the oven for about 1 hour, until firm and a skewer inserted into the center comes out clean. Arrange the peppermint wafers neatly over the top and return to the oven for 2–3 minutes until just melted. Allow to cool completely in the pan, then remove and wrap. Store for 24 hours.

To serve, cut into 16 equal portions. If you can leave them alone, these brownies will keep for about a week in an airtight container.

Flourless mint chocolate brownies

Blondies

Blondies

Vanilla

If the familiar bitter chocolate bar is called a brownie, then it makes sense that a white chocolate version is a blondie. Be warned, they're very moreish!

Makes 16

12oz (350g) **white chocolate,** broken into small pieces

¾ stick (90g) **butter**

4 **eggs,** beaten

¾ cup (150g) **unbleached superfine sugar**

¼ cup (30g) **vanilla sugar (see tip below)**

1½ cups (180g) **self-rising flour**

1¼ cups (180g) **ground almonds**

2oz (60g) **milk chocolate**

Preheat the oven to 350°F (180°C). Grease and line with baking parchment a 7 x 11-in (18 x 28-cm) rectangular cake pan. Place 4oz (125g) white chocolate pieces in a heatproof bowl with the butter. Place the bowl over a saucepan of gently simmering water. Allow to melt then remove from the water and cool for 10 minutes.

Beat in the eggs and sugars. Sift in the flour and add the ground almonds, and carefully fold into the mixture along with 6oz (180g) chocolate pieces until well combined.

Transfer to the prepared pan and smooth over the top. Bake in the oven for about 40 minutes until risen, firm and golden. Allow to cool in the pan, then cut into 16 pieces. Carefully remove from the pan and transfer to a wire rack.

Melt the remaining white chocolate and the milk chocolate separately. Spoon a little of the two chocolates onto each slice and gently mix together, using a skewer, to give a marbled effect. Allow to set before serving.

■ *To make vanilla sugar, simply add a couple of vanilla pods to a jar of sugar. Within a day or so the sugar will have become infused with the scent of vanilla.*

Double chocolate cookies

Snack-time favorite

When it comes to comfort food, nothing beats a freshly-baked chocolate cookie. These soft-bake treats are quick and easy to make – and you'll be asked to serve them again and again.

Makes 24

1½ sticks (180g) **butter, softened**
1 cup (150g) **light brown sugar**
1 **egg**
1⅔ cups (225g) **all-purpose flour**
¼ cup (30g) **cocoa powder**
Pinch **of salt**
½ tsp **baking powder**
¾ cup (150g) **milk chocolate chunks**

Preheat the oven to 375°F (190°C). In a bowl, cream together the butter and sugar until pale and creamy. Beat in the egg.

Sift in the flour, cocoa, salt and baking powder. Add the chocolate chunks and mix well to form a soft dough.

Drop heaped teaspoonfuls, spaced well apart, on large baking sheets lined with baking parchment. Press down lightly and bake for about 12 minutes until spread and just set. Cool on the sheets for about 10 minutes until beginning to firm up, then transfer to a wire rack. Best served warm.

Double chocolate cookies

Chocolate and prune macaroon bars

Almondy

Adding prunes to a chocolate mixture enhances the chocolatey flavor and gives a moist, sticky texture which improves on storing. Use soft prunes and they will practically disappear in the mixture.

Makes 16

1¼ cups (250g) **pitted no-need-to-soak prunes,** finely chopped
1 cup (250ml) **cold water**
½ cup (60g) **cocoa powder**
1 stick (125g) **butter**
1¼ cups (250g) **dark brown sugar**
2 **eggs,** beaten
½ tsp **almond extract**
1¼ cups (180g) **ground almonds**
1 tsp **baking soda**
¼ tsp **baking powder**
½ **quantity Bitter chocolate fudge frosting (see page 162)**

Preheat the oven to 350°F (180°C). Grease and line with baking parchment a 7 x 11-in (18 x 28-cm) oblong cake pan. Put the prunes, water, cocoa, butter and sugar in a large saucepan, and heat gently until the butter melts, the sugar dissolves and the mixture is dark and molasses-like. Remove from the heat and cool for 10 minutes.

Stir in the remaining ingredients except the frosting and then pour into the prepared pan. Smooth the top and bake in the oven for about 45 minutes until firm to the touch and a skewer inserted into the center comes out clean. Allow to cool in the pan, then remove and wrap. Store for 24 hours before serving.

To serve, spread the Bitter chocolate fudge frosting over the chocolate bake. Cut into 16 bars.

Fruity chocolate cereal bars

Flavorful

A chewy bar that packs a punch of flavor and has a wholesome texture. These would make a great treat for a lunch box.

Makes 12

⅓ cup (60g) **golden raisins**
½ cup (60g) **no-need-to-soak dried apricots,** finely chopped
1½ cups (180g) **all-purpose flour**
Pinch **of salt**
Scant 1¼ cups (125g) **steel-cut oats**
½ cup (125g) **milk or semisweet chocolate chunks**
1 stick (100g) **unsalted butter or** ½ cup (100g) **margarine**
Scant ½ cup (100g) **superfine sugar**
3 Tbsp **corn syrup**

Preheat the oven to 350°F (180°C). Grease and line with baking parchment a 7-in (18-cm) square cake pan. In a mixing bowl, mix together the raisins, apricots, flour, salt, oats and chocolate chunks.

In a small saucepan, gently melt together the butter, sugar and syrup without boiling. Cool for 10 minutes, then stir into the dry ingredients until well mixed and coated in the melted butter syrup.

Press into the prepared pan and bake in the oven for about 30 minutes until lightly golden. Cut into 12 bars and allow to cool in the pan.

Mini orange brioche surprises

Mini orange brioche surprises

Zesty

A lovely breakfast treat. Serve warm so that when you tear them open they ooze with melted chocolate. Delicious with marmalade for extra zing.

Makes 4

2 cups (250g) **white hard-wheat flour**
½ tsp **salt**
1 Tbsp **superfine sugar**
1¼ tsp **instant or fast-acting dried yeast**
½ tsp finely grated **orange zest**
¼ cup (30g) **candied orange peel,** finely chopped
3 Tbsp **whole milk,** slightly warm
2 **eggs, beaten**
½ stick (60g) **unsalted butter,** melted
4 **pieces** (approx. 1oz/30g) **semisweet chocolate**
1 **egg yolk mixed with** 1 Tbsp **cold water, to glaze**

Sift the flour, salt and superfine sugar into a bowl and stir in the dried yeast, orange zest and orange peel. Make a well in the center.

Mix together the milk and beaten egg with the melted butter and pour into the center of the well. Mix the ingredients together with your fingers, then tip onto a lightly-floured work surface, bring together and knead lightly for about 5 minutes until you have a dough slightly softer than a pastry mixture. Lightly flour the bowl and place the dough back in it. Cover loosely and set in a warm place for about an hour until doubled in size.

Gently reknead the dough to form a smooth ball. Cut into four equal portions, flatten and place a piece of chocolate in the center of each. Bring the dough up around the chocolate and form into a ball. If you have four 4-in (10-cm) individual brioche pans, grease them and place a dough ball in each, otherwise greased muffin pans will work just as well. Cover loosely with lightly-oiled clear food wrap and leave in a warm place for about 45 minutes until doubled in size. Preheat the oven to 400°F (200°C).

Glaze the brioche with the beaten egg yolk mixture and bake in the oven for 20–25 minutes until risen and richly golden. Transfer to a wire rack to cool slightly. Serve warm.

Hot puddings

I have to be honest now: I rarely choose a chocolate pudding when it comes to dessert. Not because I don't like them, it's usually because I'm too full and I find the chocolate too rich to enjoy it properly. I prefer to savor my chocolate as a meal on its own – very naughty but ever so nice – and that way I can enjoy the chocolate experience to the maximum!

I do have several friends who always have a chocolate pudding, so this chapter's dedicated to them – and they know who they are! I've put some real rib-sticking, "proper" puddings in this chapter, alongside lighter choices, so you should find something to suit every occasion.

For a filling treat why not try the Chocolate, molasses and ginger pudding with a generous serving of chocolate custard, or the thick and creamy Chocolate risotto – both guaranteed to hit the spot on a cold day. The bitter chocolate espresso soufflé is a much lighter option and packed with flavor. If you want to serve something very different to your guests, serve them a bowl of Fragrant chocolate soup – it's full of exotic flavors and gives a real chocolate "hit" after a meal. I'm sure it'll be a real talking point.

Fragrant chocolate soup

Fragrant chocolate soup

Exotic

Really a variation on a chocolate fondue, this rich, dark recipe has a citrus edge. It's best served warm for maximum flavor, and will thicken as it cools. Serve in small amounts.

Serves 6

2 stalks lemongrass
1 lime
2 star anise
4 Tbsp light brown sugar
14-oz (400-ml) can coconut milk
2oz (60g) unsweetened or 85%
    (or above) cocoa bitter chocolate,
    grated
⅔ cup (150ml) heavy cream
2oz (60g) milk chocolate, grated
Finely shredded lime zest,
    to decorate

Trim the stalk from the lemongrass, split the bulb in half and place in a saucepan. Using a vegetable peeler, pare off the rind from the lime into the saucepan. Extract the juice and set aside.

Add the star anise and sugar to the saucepan and stir in the coconut milk. Slowly bring to a boil, then turn off the heat, cover and allow to infuse for 30 minutes. Stir in the lime juice, then pour the mixture through a strainer and set aside.

When ready to serve, put the unsweetened chocolate in a saucepan with the cream. Heat very gently to melt the chocolate and mix well to make a paste. Gradually stir in the infused coconut milk and heat through, without boiling, until hot.

Pour into small warm cups or ramekins and sprinkle with grated milk chocolate and lime zest. Serve immediately.

Spiced molten puddings

Oozing

These puddings have become popular on the menus of trendy restaurants. They are very easy to make and can be prepared in advance and cooked just before serving.

Serves 4

4oz (125g) **unsweetened or 85% (or above) cocoa bitter chocolate**
1 stick (125g) **unsalted butter,** cut into small pieces
2 **eggs,** beaten
2 **egg yolks**
4 Tbsp **superfine sugar**
½ tsp **ground cinnamon**
2 tsp **all-purpose flour**
4 **small pieces white chocolate**
2 tsp **confectioner's sugar**
1 tsp **cocoa powder**
Light cream, to serve

Preheat the oven to 450°F (230°C). Grease and lightly flour four ⅔-cup (150-ml) custard cups or ramekins. Break the unsweetened chocolate into pieces and place in a heatproof bowl with the butter. Set over a pan of gently simmering water and allow to melt, then remove from the water and set aside.

Meanwhile, whisk the eggs, egg yolks and sugar together until thick and creamy. Whisk in the warm melted chocolate, and stir in the cinnamon and flour to make a thick batter.

Divide the mixture among the prepared cups. Push a piece of white chocolate into the center of each pudding. Place the cups on a baking sheet and cook in the oven for 6–8 minutes until the sides are set but the middle is still wobbly – insert a toothpick carefully into the center to check that the white chocolate has melted.

Immediately invert the puddings onto warmed serving plates and let stand, still in the cups, for 30 seconds before removing. Serve immediately dusted with confectioner's sugar and then cocoa, accompanied with light cream.

■ *If you aren't ready to cook the puddings right away, cover them and put in the fridge for up to 24 hours. When you are ready to cook the puddings, let them warm to room temperature.*

Spiced molten puddings

Bitter chocolate espresso soufflé

Airy

The secret of soufflé-making is to be organized. Your wonderful creation needs to be served as soon as it comes out of the oven, before it sinks. So while it's baking, get your serving tools ready!

Serves 6

4oz (125g) **70% cocoa bitter chocolate**
2 Tbsp **cold water**
½ stick (60g) **unsalted butter**
⅓ cup (45g) **all-purpose flour**
⅔ cup (150ml) **whole milk**
½ cup (100ml) **cold espresso coffee**
5 **large eggs,** separated
Scant ¼ cup (30g) **superfine sugar**
2 tsp **confectioner's sugar**
1 **quantity Coffee cream sauce (see page 158), to serve**

Preheat the oven to 375°F (190°C) and place a baking sheet in the oven. Grease the base and sides of a 6¼-cup (1.5-L) soufflé dish. Break the chocolate into pieces and place in a small heatproof bowl with the cold water. Set over a pan of gently simmering water and allow to melt, then remove from the water and set aside.

Meanwhile, melt the butter in a saucepan and blend in the flour. Cook for 1 minute then remove from the heat and gradually blend in the milk and cold coffee. Return to the heat and gently bring to a boil, stirring, until very thick and glossy. Cool for 10 minutes then beat in the melted chocolate, egg yolks and sugar.

In a large grease-free bowl, whisk the egg whites until stiff. Fold a quarter of the egg whites into the chocolate mixture to loosen it, then spoon the chocolate mixture over the remaining whites and fold in carefully.

Turn into the prepared dish. Set on the preheated baking sheet and bake in the oven for about 40 minutes until risen and firm on the top.

As soon as the soufflé is cooked, dust with confectioner's sugar and serve with hot Coffee cream sauce.

Chocolate risotto

Contemporary

If you're looking to serve a rich, rib-sticking pudding, this is the one. It's really a posh rice pudding, and is very rich and chocolatey, and very, very yummy.

Serves 6–8

5½ cups (1.3L) **whole milk**
1 **vanilla pod,** split
½ stick (60g) **unsalted butter**
3 cups (400g) **arborio rice**
6 Tbsp **superfine sugar**
2oz (60g) **unsweetened or 85%
  (or above) cocoa bitter chocolate,
  grated**
4 Tbsp **heavy cream**
Scant ½ cup (60g) **semisweet
  chocolate chips**
6 Tbsp **mascarpone cheese,
  to serve**
1 tsp **cocoa powder, to dust**

Pour the milk in a saucepan. Bring to a boil. Remove from the heat, add the vanilla pod and leave to infuse for 30 minutes. Discard the pod.

In another saucepan, melt the butter and gently stir in the rice until well coated. Add a ladleful of the vanilla milk and cook gently, stirring, until absorbed. Stir in the sugar.

Continue adding small quantities of milk and cooking until it is absorbed, until all the milk is used up and the rice is swollen and tender and the mixture is thick and creamy – this will take about 30 minutes. Stir in the grated chocolate and cream and heat through for a further minute until the chocolate is melted.

To serve, stir in the chocolate chips and pile into warmed serving bowls. Serve each with a spoonful of mascarpone on top and a light dusting of cocoa powder. Serve immediately.

Chocolate, molasses and ginger pudding

Dark

Steamed pudding is a great comforter on a cold winter's day, and this one is flavored with the warming power of ginger. Best served with my Chocolate custard sauce.

Serves 8

3oz (90g) **70% cocoa bitter chocolate**
1½ sticks (180g) **unsalted butter**
Scant 1¼ cups (180g) **molasses sugar or dark brown sugar**
3 **eggs,** beaten
2 Tbsp **whole milk**
¼ cup (30g) **preserved ginger, finely chopped**
1½ cups (180g) **self-rising flour**
1 tsp **ground ginger**
Chocolate custard sauce (see page 160), to serve

Grease a 5½-cup (1.2-L) soufflé dish and place a small disc of baking parchment in the bottom.

Break the chocolate into pieces and place in a small heatproof bowl over a pan of gently simmering water and allow to melt, then remove from the water and set aside.

Meanwhile, cream together the butter and sugar in a bowl, until paler, thick and creamy. Gradually whisk in the eggs, milk and melted chocolate, and stir in the chopped ginger.

Sift the flour and ground ginger into the bowl and carefully fold into the chocolate mixture. Spoon into the prepared dish and smooth the top. Top the pudding with a circle of baking parchment, and then cover the top of the soufflé dish with a layer of foil, folded into pleats. Secure with string.

Half fill a large saucepan with water and bring to a boil. Either place the pudding in a steamer compartment over the saucepan or stand on a trivet in the saucepan. Cover tightly with a lid and steam for 2 hours, topping the water level up as required, until the pudding is risen and firm to the touch – a skewer inserted into the center of the pudding should come out clean.

To serve, unwrap the pudding and invert onto a warmed serving plate. Serve at once with hot Chocolate custard sauce.

Chocolate, molasses and ginger pudding

Chocolate and banana upside down pudding

Sticky-sweet

Chocolate and bananas go together very well, and in this pudding, the bananas cook to a soft tenderness in a toffee syrup. Choose ripe bananas for best results.

Serves 8

2 sticks (225g) **unsalted butter**
2 cups (275g) **light brown sugar**
3 **large ripe bananas**
4 **eggs,** beaten
1 tsp **vanilla extract**
1½ cups (180g) **self-rising flour**
⅛ cup (15g) **cocoa powder**
½ tsp **ground cinnamon**
Pinch **salt**
**Chocolate cream sauce
    (see page 159), to serve**

Preheat the oven to 350°F (180°C). Melt 1 stick (100g) butter in a saucepan and, when bubbling, add 1 cup (150g) of the sugar. Simmer gently for about 3 minutes, stirring occasionally, until syrupy. Pour into the base of a 9-in (23-cm) round cake pan.

Peel the bananas; cut two in half, and then slice through lengthwise. Fan the banana slices in a circle in the base of the pan. Set aside. Mash the remaining banana.

In a mixing bowl, cream together the remaining butter and sugar until pale in color and fluffy in texture. Gradually whisk in the eggs with the vanilla and half the flour. Sift in the remaining flour, ground cinnamon and salt. Fold in, along with the mashed banana, until well mixed. Pile this mixture on top of the sliced bananas.

Smooth over the top and bake in the oven for 40–45 minutes until lightly golden and firm to the touch. Cool in the pan for 10 minutes, before turning out onto a warmed serving plate and serve immediately, banana-side up, with hot Chocolate cream sauce.

Chocolate, pear and walnut crumble

Nutty

By adding cocoa to a crumble topping, you can transform a quite ordinary pudding into something much more sophisticated. This topping also goes well with apricots or a raspberry and apple filling.

Serves 6

1½lb (750g) **ripe pears**
Finely grated **rind and juice**
   of 1 **lemon**
¼ cup (60g) + 1 Tbsp **unbleached**
   superfine sugar
1½ cups (165g) **self-rising flour**
⅛ cup (15g) **cocoa powder**
1 stick (125g) **butter**, cut into
   small pieces
½ cup (60g) **ground walnuts**
Scant ¼ cup (15g) **walnut pieces**
Chocolate custard sauce
   (see page 160), to serve

Preheat the oven to 400°F (200°C). Peel and core the pears and cut into quarters if small, or small chunks if using large pears. Place in a 5½-cup (1.2-L) oval or round pie dish and sprinkle with the lemon rind, juice and 1 Tbsp sugar. Set aside.

Sift the flour and cocoa into a bowl and rub in the butter until well combined and the mixture starts to cling together in lumps. Stir in the remaining sugar and the ground walnuts.

Set the pie dish on a baking sheet, and carefully sprinkle the crumble topping evenly over the fruit. Sprinkle with walnut pieces and bake in the oven for about 55 minutes – covering the top with foil if it looks to be darkening too much – until the pears are tender (pierce the pears in the center of the dish to check). Best served hot with hot Chocolate custard sauce.

Chocolate crêpes with white chocolate and mango

Chocolate crêpes with white chocolate and mango

Sophisticated

These crêpes are well worth the effort and are guaranteed to impress. Try them with fresh raspberries and raspberry flavored fruit sauce.

Serves 6

1 quantity **Chocolate cream sauce** made with bitter chocolate (see page 159)
1 quantity **mango Fruit sauce** (see page 160)
1 cup (125g) **all-purpose flour**
1 Tbsp **cocoa powder**
⅛ cup (30g) **superfine sugar**
Pinch **salt**
2 **eggs** + 2 **egg yolks**
1¼ cups (300ml) **whole milk**
¾ stick (75g) **unsalted butter,** melted
1 **large ripe mango,** stoned, peeled and sliced in strips, **to serve**
Grated chocolate, to serve

Make the Chocolate cream sauce and Fruit sauce. Set aside.

Sift the flour, cocoa, sugar and salt into a bowl. Make a well in the center, break in the eggs and add the extra yolks. Add half the milk and gradually work into the flour using a whisk. Beat until smooth, taking care not to overmix.

Add the remaining milk gradually, along with all but 1 Tbsp (60g) butter, whisking all the time. Beat until the ingredients are well combined. Cover

and leave in a cool place for 30 minutes. Stir the batter before using.

Lightly brush a 6-in (15-cm) crêpe pan with a little of the remaining melted butter. Pour about ¼ cup (50ml) batter into the pan, tilting the pan to coat the base thinly. Place the pan over a moderate heat and cook for about 1 minute until the crêpe begins to curl away from the pan. Slide a palette knife under the crêpe and flip it over. Cook the underside for a further minute.

Turn out onto a wire rack lined with a clean tea towel and baking parchment. Fold the paper and towel over the crêpe to keep it moist. Continue to make a further 11 crêpes, brushing the pan with melted butter as necessary, and stacking the cooked crêpes between sheets of parchment, until ready to serve.

To serve, reheat the Chocolate cream sauce. Place a few strips of mango on each crêpe and roll up tightly. Arrange two per person on warmed serving plates. Pour over some Chocolate cream sauce and then some Fruit sauce, and decorate with grated chocolate. Serve warm.

Chocolate allspice doughnuts

Sugar and spice

These doughy, sugar-coated morsels make a real treat for pudding if you serve them with the Chocolate fondue for dipping. A fruity sauce, like the one on page 160, would also work nicely. Great for parties.

Makes 16

1 **quantity Chocolate fondue (see page 164)**
1½ cups (180g) **hard-wheat all-purpose flour**
1¼ cups (150g) **all-purpose flour**
¼ cup (30g) **cocoa powder**
½ tsp **salt**
½ stick (60g) **unsalted butter**
Scant 1 cup (180g) **superfine sugar**
2 tsp **instant or fast-acting dried yeast**
Scant 1 cup (200ml) **whole milk, slightly warm (105–115°F)**
Sunflower oil, for deep-frying
½ tsp **ground allspice**

Make the Chocolate fondue and set aside.

Sift the flours, cocoa powder and salt into a mixing bowl and rub in the butter until the mixture resembles breadcrumbs. Stir in ⅓ cup (60g) sugar and the yeast. Make a well in the center and gradually blend in the milk to form a soft dough. Cover loosely and set in a warm place for about an hour or until doubled in size.

Turn the dough onto a lightly-floured surface and knead until smooth. Divide into 16 equal portions and form each into a ball. Push a greased wooden spoon handle through the center of each, wiggling the spoon to create a hole. Set aside on a lightly-greased tray while heating the oil.

Heat the oil for deep-frying in a large saucepan to 325°F (160°C) and cook the doughnuts in batches of five or six for 7–8 minutes, turning occasionally, until they are puffy and crisp. Drain well and keep warm in a shallow dish while cooking all the doughnuts.

Mix the remaining superfine sugar with the allspice and then sprinkle over the warm doughnuts, turning them to make sure they are well coated. Serve warm with the Chocolate fondue.

Chocolate allspice doughnuts

Chocolate Italian bread pudding

Comforting

Panettone is a sweet, fruity bread from Italy that is traditionally eaten at New Year. You could use brioche or a sweet cinnamon bread if preferred.

Serves 6

Scant ¼ stick (15g) **unsalted butter,** softened
Scant ½ cup (60g) **candied citrus rind,** finely chopped
3oz (90g) **70% cocoa bitter chocolate,** grated
2 cups (450ml) **light cream**
6 **thick slices cut from a 1-lb (500-g) panettone** (about 12oz/350g)
3 **eggs,** beaten
4 Tbsp **superfine sugar**
Finely grated **rind** 1 **orange**
¼ cup (30g) **pine nuts,** toasted
½ tsp **ground cinnamon**
Light cream, to serve

Preheat the oven to 350°F (180°C). Thickly butter a 6¼-cup (1.5-L) ovenproof gratin dish. Sprinkle the candied rind on the bottom of the dish. Set aside.

Place the chocolate and cream in a saucepan. Heat very gently, stirring, until the chocolate melts – do not allow to boil – and then remove from the heat and set aside.

Meanwhile, cut the panettone into small cubes and pack into the prepared dish.

Whisk together the eggs and 2 Tbsp sugar until pale and frothy, and pour over the chocolate cream. Mix well and strain through a sieve. Stir in the orange rind and pour over the bread. Stand for 30 minutes to soak.

Place the gratin dish in a roasting pan and pour sufficient water into the roasting pan to come halfway up the side of the dish. Sprinkle the pudding with pine nuts and bake for 40–45 minutes until the blade of a knife inserted in the center of the pudding comes out clean. Mix the remaining sugar with the cinnamon and sprinkle over the top of the pudding. Serve hot with light cream.

Chocolate orange surprise pudding

Comforting

This is a delicious recipe I remember from my childhood. Miraculously, a rich chocolate sauce appears at the bottom of the dish once the pudding is cooked.

Serves 4–6

½ stick (60g) **butter, softened**
Scant ¾ cup (90g) **light brown sugar**
2 **eggs, separated**
⅓ cup (45g) **self rising flour**
1 tsp **finely grated orange rind**
5 tsp **cocoa powder**
1½ cups (350ml) **whole milk**

Preheat the oven to 350°F (180°C). Grease a 4½-cup (1-L) ovenproof dish.

In a bowl, cream together the butter and sugar until pale, thick and creamy. Beat in the egg yolks.

Sift the flour and cocoa powder into the bowl and carefully fold into the chocolate mixture along with the orange rind. Gradually stir in the milk to make a smooth, thick batter.

In a grease-free bowl, whisk the egg whites until stiff and fold into the mixture. Spoon into the prepared dish and smooth the top. Stand on a baking sheet and cook for 35–45 minutes until the top is set and spongy to the touch – this pudding will separate into a chocolate sauce layer with a sponge topping. Serve hot with custard.

Chilled desserts

This is probably the most diverse recipe section in the book because there's such a variety of tastes and textures. But they do all have one thing in common – lots of chocolate. Another good thing about many of these recipes is that they don't have to be saved for meal times; you could easily have a slice of cheesecake with your morning coffee or a piece of roulade for an afternoon snack. Now you know even more about my eating habits!

A lot of people choose chocolate ice cream as their favorite chilled chocolate dessert so I've included an easy method that splits into three chocolate flavors: white, milk and bitter; or if you prefer, you can make a bigger batch of your chosen variety. If you're on a dairy-free diet you might like to try the Bitter chocolate sorbet instead of ice cream; it's very rich and full of chocolate taste. If you're a real ice-cream lover, then there's a recipe for a chocolate sundae and a trifle.

For the height of chocolate sophistication, there are two recipes definitely worth pointing out: the Three chocolate terrine is one of the simplest and yet most attractive desserts to make, whereas the Chocolate marquise is a classic, bitter chocolate recipe for the real connoisseur.

Bitter chocolate sorbet

Silky smooth

Not quite as rich as ice cream, but this chiller has a big chocolate hit. The sugar syrup means that it melts quite quickly so don't take it out of the freezer too far in advance.

Serves 6

1 **quantity plain Sugar syrup (see page 158)**
½ cup (60g) **cocoa powder**
1 **vanilla pod,** split
Chocolate ginger snaps (see page 167), to serve

Make the sugar syrup. When the syrup has boiled, sift the cocoa powder into a heatproof bowl and blend in a little of the syrup to make a paste, and then stir the paste into the rest of the syrup until well blended. Add the vanilla pod and set aside to cool completely.

Discard the vanilla pod and, if you have one, churn the mixture in an ice-cream maker until frozen. Store in the freezer until required. Alternatively, pour the mixture into a freezer-proof container and freeze until just beginning to set around the edges, approximately 1–1½ hours. Take out of the freezer and whisk well to break down the ice crystals evenly. Return to the freezer and freeze for a further 1½–2 hours, whisking every 30 minutes, until firm. Cover and store in the freezer until required.

To serve, set at room temperature for about 5 minutes and scoop into small serving dishes. Serve with Chocolate ginger snaps.

■ *You can make a mocha version of this sorbet by adding 2 tsp instant coffee granules to the syrup when you add the extra cocoa powder. Instead of vanilla you could try using a cinnamon stick, 3 star anise or 4 crushed cardamom pods.*

Bitter chocolate sorbet

Mocha cream jello

Mocha cream jello

Grown-up

A jello might not be the first thing you think of for pudding, unless you're a child, but these creations are well worth considering. The alcohol is optional – you could add a nut syrup instead.

Serves 4

½ **quantity Chocolate sugar syrup (see page 158)**
½ cup (100ml) **espresso coffee, chilled**
½ cup (100ml) **light cream**
4 Tbsp **brandy (optional)**
4 Tbsp cold **water**
¼oz packet **granulated gelatin**
Roasted **coffee beans and chocolate mix powder, to serve**

Make up the Chocolate sugar syrup and set aside to cool. Stir in the coffee, light cream and brandy, if using.

Place 4 Tbsp cold water in a small heatproof bowl. Prepare gelatin according to the packet instructions. Set the bowl over a saucepan of simmering water and heat the gelatin gently until dissolved. Alternatively, heat in the microwave for about 25 seconds on high. Do not allow to boil as this prevents a proper set taking place.

Stir the liquid gelatin into the mocha mixture and pour into four coffee cups or serving dishes. Leave to set in the fridge for at least 2 hours.

To serve, top each with a few roasted coffee beans and a light dusting of chocolate mix powder.

Trio of chocolate ices

Divine

I'm lucky enough to have an electric ice-cream maker so I can make my own chocolate ice creams very quickly. If you don't have one, here is an easy recipe that makes a fondant-style ice cream that requires no beating.

Serves 6

1 **quantity plain Sugar syrup (see page 158)**
2½oz (75g) **unsweetened or 85% (or above) cocoa bitter chocolate,** grated
2½oz (75g) **milk chocolate,** grated
2½oz (75g) **white chocolate,** grated
Few drops **vanilla extract**
1¾ cups (400g) **full-fat cream cheese**
⅔ cups (150ml) **heavy cream**

Make the plain Sugar syrup. When it has boiled, divide equally between three heatproof bowls. Stir a different grated chocolate into each bowl, whisking until melted. Set aside to cool. Add a few drops of vanilla extract to the white chocolate syrup.

Once the syrups have cooled, taking each chocolate syrup separately, blend a little syrup into one-third of the soft cheese and then whisk in the remaining syrup. Lightly whip the cream and fold one-third into each chocolate mixture.

Transfer to three small freezer containers, cover and put in the coldest part of the freezer for at least 4 hours until firmly frozen. Let stand at room temperature for about 20 minutes before scooping some of each flavor into individual serving bowls.

White chocolate and ginger cheesecake

Zingy

A very simple cheesecake that's rich and satisfying. In order to get a smooth texture, make sure the chocolate is still warm when you add it to the other ingredients.

Serves 10

12oz (350g) **ginger cookies,** finely crushed

1 Tbsp **cocoa powder**

1 stick (125g) **unsalted butter,** melted

8oz (250g) **white chocolate,** broken into pieces

1¼ cups (300g) **full-fat cream cheese, at room temperature**

¼ cup (45g) **preserved ginger in syrup,** finely chopped, **plus**

2 Tbsp **of the ginger syrup**

1 cup (250ml) **heavy cream, at room temperature**

2oz (60g) **semisweet chocolate,** grated

Grease and base-line with baking parchment a deep 9-in (23-cm) springform cake pan. Place the crushed cookies in a bowl and sift over the cocoa powder. Pour the melted butter over the cookies and cocoa and bind together. Press onto the base and sides of the pan using the back of a metal spoon. Chill until required.

Place chocolate pieces in a heatproof bowl and melt over a pan of barely simmering water, and set aside. In a large mixing bowl, beat together the cream cheese, chopped ginger and heavy cream.

Fold in the warm white chocolate and spoon the mixture over the cookie base. Smooth the top and chill for 2–3 hours until set.

To serve, release the cheesecake from the pan and place on a serving plate. Sprinkle with grated chocolate and serve.

Chocolate crème brûlée

Chocolate crème brûlée

Velvety smooth

A much-loved French creation, consisting of a creamy chocolate custard topped with a crunchy, crisp sugar topping. Serve with my Chocolate shortbread to dip (see page 168).

Serves 6

2½ cups (600ml) **whipping cream**
2oz (60g) **unsweetened or 85% (or above) cocoa bitter chocolate,** grated
1 **vanilla pod,** split
4 **egg yolks**
Scant 1 cup (180g) **superfine sugar**

Preheat the oven to 300°F (150°C). Pour the cream into a saucepan and add the grated chocolate. Heat gently, without boiling, stirring, until hot and the chocolate has melted. Remove from the heat. Add the vanilla pod to the hot cream and leave to infuse for 30 minutes. Discard the pod.

Meanwhile, whisk the egg yolks and ¼ cup (60g) sugar together in a bowl until thick, pale and creamy. Pour over the chocolate cream, stirring gently until well mixed.

Set six ⅔-cup (150-ml) ramekins in a roasting pan and pour the custard mixture slowly into the ramekins, dividing it equally among them. Pour sufficient hot water into the roasting pan to come halfway up the sides of the ramekins.

Bake in the oven for about 1 hour or until set – the blade of a knife inserted into the center should come out clean when cooked. Remove from the pan and cool completely before chilling for at least 3 hours.

Preheat the grill to its hottest setting. Sprinkle the remaining sugar thickly over the top of each custard. Cook for 3–5 minutes until the sugar turns to caramel. Chill for a further 2 hours before serving.

Three chocolate terrine

Impressive

Your friends will think this has taken you hours to prepare, when really it's one of the easiest layered desserts I've come across. It's very rich, so serve it in thin slices.

Serves 8

4oz (125g) **white chocolate**
4oz (125g) **milk chocolate**
4oz (125g) **70% cocoa bitter chocolate**
Few drops **vanilla extract**
1¾ cups (450ml) **heavy cream, at room temperature**
1 cup (250g) **fresh raspberries, to serve**
1 **quantity raspberry Fruit sauce (see page 160)**

Line a 2¼-cup (500-g) loaf pan with clear food wrap. Break the chocolate into pieces and place each type in a small heatproof bowl and melt over saucepans of barely simmering water. Remove only the white chocolate from the water and add a few drops of vanilla extract. Leave the other two bowls of chocolate on the water, but off the heat, to keep them molton. Set aside.

Lightly whip the cream until just peaking and fold one-third into the white chocolate. Transfer to the prepared pan and smooth the surface.

Chill for about 30 minutes until firm. While this is chilling, cover the cream and set aside in a cool place – try to avoid chilling the cream unless the air temperature is very warm.

When the white chocolate is set, mix half of the remaining cream with the melted milk chocolate and spread on top of the white chocolate until smooth. Chill once more for about 30 minutes until firm.

Finally, remelt the bitter chocolate if necessary. Mix with the remaining cream and spread on top of the milk chocolate layer. Smooth the surface, cover and chill for at least 4 hours until completely set.

To serve, invert the pan onto a serving plate and peel off the clear food wrap. Arrange fresh raspberries around the edge of the terrine and serve in slices with the raspberry Fruit sauce.

■ *You will find the chocolate and cream will stiffen considerably when mixed together, so try and keep the chocolate slightly warm and the cream at room temperature for even mixing and a smooth finished texture.*

Three chocolate terrine

Iced chocolate cherry trifle

Contemporary

Usually I'm not a great trifle lover, but I have to admit that this one is rather good. If you crave a more traditional version, simply replace the ice cream with chocolate or vanilla custard.

Serves 8

1 **quantity Chocolate trifle sponge** (see page 165) or six ½-in (1-cm) thick slices ready-made chocolate pound cake
1½ cups (500g) **pitted canned cherries in light syrup,** drained, reserving 4 or 8 Tbsp **syrup (see below)**
4 Tbsp **cherry brandy or Kirsch** (optional)
1 **quantity bitter Chocolate cream sauce (see page 159)**
1 **quantity bitter chocolate ice cream** (see page 120) or 2¼ cups (500g) ready-made chocolate ice cream
1¼ cups (300ml) **whipping cream**
Chocolate decorations of your choice, to decorate

Cut the sponge or cake into bite-sized pieces and arrange in the bottom of a large glass serving dish. Spoon over the drained cherries and, if using the brandy or Kirsch, spoon it over the cherries along with 4 Tbsp reserved juice. If you're omitting the alcohol spoon over 8 Tbsp reserved juice. Cover and chill until required.

Make the bitter Chocolate cream sauce. Allow to cool until it is beginning to set, but don't let it set completely otherwise you won't be able to pour it over the trifle.

Scoop the ice cream over the cherries to cover them. Pour the chocolate sauce over the ice cream – it will start to set quickly, so pour it over evenly. Whip the cream until softly peaking and pile on top. Cover and chill for up to 2 hours before serving – it will start to melt if left too long. Decorate and serve as soon as possible (see pages 22–28 for decoration ideas).

Petits pots au chocolat

Powerful

One of the all-time classic chocolate desserts from France. These dense, custard-like mousses are rich and should really hit the spot if you're passionate about chocolate.

Serves 8

1¾ cups (450ml) **whole milk**
3½oz (100g) **unsweetened or 85% (or above) cocoa bitter chocolate,** grated
4 **egg yolks**
Generous ¼ cup (60g) **superfine sugar**
4 Tbsp grated **semisweet chocolate and** 8 **chocolate coffee dragées to serve**

Preheat the oven to 325°F (160°C). Arrange eight ½-cup (100-ml) ramekins or French custard pots in a roasting pan and set aside. Pour the milk into a saucepan and bring to just below boiling point. Remove from the heat and stir in the chocolate until melted.

Whisk together the egg yolks with the sugar until pale, thick and creamy. Pour over the hot chocolate milk, stirring constantly. Pour the mixture through a sieve into a heatproof batter bowl. Divide the chocolate custard mixture among the ramekins or custard pots. Pour sufficient hot water into the roasting pan to come halfway up the sides of the ramekins. Bake in the oven for 25–35 minutes, depending on the size of the ramekin, until just set but still slightly soft in the center. Test by inserting a round-bladed knife in the center – it should be thickly coated in the custard to be ready. Remove from the pan and allow to cool, then chill for at least 2 hours.

Allow the chocolate pots to stand at room temperature for about 20 minutes before serving. Sprinkle with grated chocolate and top with a chocolate coffee dragée.

Pecan caramel chocolate roulade

Pecan caramel chocolate roulade

Luscious

A great combination of textures and flavors. You can make the roulade base up in advance, but the roulade is better assembled close to serving as the nut brittle will start to dissolve if refrigerated for too long.

Serves 8

6 **large eggs,** separated
¾ cup (150g) **superfine sugar**
½ cup (60g) **cocoa powder**
6oz (180g) **milk chocolate**
1 cup (250g) **mascarpone cheese**
1 **quantity pecan Nut brittle
(see page 168),** crushed
⅔ cup (150ml) **whipping cream,**
whipped
**Cocoa powder and confectioner's
sugar, to dust**

Preheat the oven to 350°F (180°C). Grease a 13 x 9-in (33 x 23-cm) jelly roll pan. Cut a piece of baking parchment about 2in (5cm) larger all around than the pan. Press the parchment into the pan, creasing to fit the sides. Cut the parchment at the corners of the pan and overlap the cut paper to fit snugly.

In a large bowl, whisk the egg yolks and sugar until very thick and pale. Sift in the cocoa powder, and using a large metal spoon, fold the ingredients into each other.

In another bowl, whisk the egg whites until just stiff but not dry and fold these into the mixture. Pour into the prepared pan and smooth the surface. Bake in the middle of the oven for 20 minutes until springy to the touch. Take care not to overcook. Allow to cool in the pan – it will sink on cooling!

When the sponge is cool, break the chocolate in pieces and place in a heatproof bowl over a saucepan of barely simmering water until melted. Remove from the water and set aside. Turn the sponge onto a large sheet of baking parchment and peel away the lining paper. Spread the melted chocolate evenly over the surface, then carefully spread over the mascarpone cheese. Sprinkle the Nut brittle on top.

Working quickly, taking hold of one short end of the parchment, use it to gently roll the roulade like a thick jelly roll. Pull the paper away. The roulade may crack. You should aim to roll the roulade up before the chocolate sets. Put on a serving plate, cover and chill for 30 minutes.

To serve, dust with cocoa and confectioner's sugar and cut into thick slices.

Chocolate velvet slice

Rich

This recipe takes a little time to prepare so it's a dessert for a special occasion. It looks impressive and tastes fantastic, and is worth the extra effort. The sponge trimmings can be made into cake crumbs for use in other recipes.

Serves 10

Chocolate jelly roll sponge base (see page 36)
4oz (125g) **semisweet chocolate**
1 stick (125g) **unsalted butter,** cut into small pieces
¼ cup (30g (1oz) **cocoa powder**
Scant 1 cup (200ml) **heavy cream**
2 **large eggs**
½ cup (125g) **superfine sugar**
2oz (60g) **unsweetened or 85% (or above) cocoa bitter chocolate**
2oz (60g) **milk chocolate**
Light cream or Coffee cream sauce (see page 158), to serve

Line a 4½-cup (1-kg) loaf pan with clear food wrap, allowing it to overlap the sides and ends. Make and bake the Chocolate jelly roll sponge but do not roll up; leave as a rectangular sponge base. Remove from the pan and allow to cool on a wire rack. Peel off the paper and trim away the crusts, and then cut the sponge into sufficient pieces to line the bottom and sides of the prepared loaf pan. Carefully press the sponge pieces into the pan. Set aside.

Break the semisweet chocolate into pieces and place in a heatproof bowl with the butter and melt over a saucepan of barely simmering water. Remove from the water, sift in the cocoa and mix well. Set aside.

Whisk the eggs and sugar together until pale, thick and creamy. In another bowl, whip the cream until just peaking. Gently mix both the egg and cream into the melted chocolate until well blended. Spoon into the sponge-lined pan and cover with baking parchment. Chill for at least 3 hours.

Break the bitter and milk chocolate into pieces and place in separate small heatproof bowls and melt over saucepans of barely simmering water. Remove from the water and set aside.

Invert the loaf pan onto a small board and remove the food wrap. Drizzle the melted chocolate, alternating, over the top and sides of the pan. Return to the fridge for 30 minutes.

To serve, carefully cut into slices using a large knife and serve with light cream or Coffee cream sauce.

Ultimate chocolate sundae

Fun

You can add anything sweet to a sundae and this is my idea of a perfect example – a real treat when you're feeling a bit down in the dumps.

Makes 1

Large handful **of blueberries, washed** and dried
2 **double chocolate cookies,** lightly crushed
½oz (15g) **white chocolate,** grated
2 scoops **Bitter chocolate ice cream (see page 120) or ready-made ice cream**
2 spoonfuls **Chocolate custard sauce (see page 160)**
Large **swirl of whipped cream**
½oz (15g) **milk chocolate,** grated
Drizzle **of Chocolate sugar syrup (see page 158)**

Put a few of the blueberries in the bottom of a tall sundae glass and top with some of the crushed cookies and the grated white chocolate. Add a scoop of ice cream and then a spoonful of custard.

Repeat the layers, reserving a few blueberries. Top with a swirl of whipped cream, the milk chocolate, reserved blueberries and finally some Chocolate sugar syrup. Serve immediately and eat using a long-handled spoon. Enjoy!

■ *Other good fruits to use in a chocolate sundae are chopped banana, mango, peach or pear, or fresh strawberries and raspberries. For a less calorific version, replace the ice cream with sorbet and top with plain yogurt.*

Chocolate marquise

Connoisseur

There are many variations of this darkest of chocolate desserts. The chocolate flavor is very intense, so it is best served in thin slices with sweet acid fruits.

Serves 10–12

8oz (250g) **unsweetened or 85% (or above) cocoa bitter chocolate**
1 stick (125g) **unsalted butter, softened**
1¼ cups (180g) **confectioner's sugar**
⅔ cup (150ml) **heavy cream, at room temperature**
1 tsp **instant coffee granules dissolved in** 2 tsp boiled water, cooled
1 Tbsp **cocoa powder**
Fresh sweet pineapple and Coffee cream sauce (see page 158), to serve

Line a 2¼-cup (500-g) loaf pan with clear food wrap allowing it to overlap the sides and ends. Break the chocolate in pieces and place in a heatproof bowl over a pan of barely simmering water until melted. Remove from the water and set aside.

Put the butter in a mixing bowl and sift in the confectioner's sugar. Gradually mix the two together and then beat until soft and smooth. Gradually beat in the melted chocolate. Stir in the cream and coffee mixture.

Pour into the prepared pan and smooth over the top. Cover with clear food wrap and chill for at least 4 hours until firm.

To serve, invert onto a serving plate and remove the food wrap. Stand at room temperature for about 30 minutes before serving. Dredge all over with cocoa powder and accompany with fresh pineapple and Coffee cream sauce.

■ *Other fruits that are good accompaniments to this dessert are blueberries, strawberries and raspberries.*

Chocolate marquise

Baked chocolate, rum and raisin cheesecake

Dense

A very rich and cloying textured cheesecake is hard to beat in my opinion. This one has a wonderfully creamy, dense texture that is perfectly complemented by the hint of sweet orange flavor.

Serves 8

⅓ cup (60g) **seedless raisins**
2 Tbsp **dark rum or** freshly squeezed orange juice
½ stick (60g) **unsalted butter**
6oz (180g) **double chocolate chip cookies,** crushed
2 cups (500g) **medium-fat cream cheese**
1 tsp finely grated **orange rind**
2 **eggs,** beaten
Generous ½ cup (125g) **superfine sugar**
¼ cup (30g) **cocoa powder**
Light cream and fresh orange segments, to serve

Preheat the oven to 300°F (150°C). Grease and line with baking parchment an 8-in (20-cm) springform cake pan. Place the raisins in a small bowl and spoon over the rum or orange juice. Set aside for about an hour to soak and plump up. Meanwhile, melt the butter in a saucepan. Remove from the heat and stir in the crushed cookies. Press the mixture into the base of the pan using the back of a spoon. Chill until required.

In a mixing bowl, beat the cream cheese to soften. Stir in the orange rind and whisk in the eggs and sugar. Sift in the cocoa powder and carefully stir in along with the soaked raisins and liquid until well mixed.

Transfer to the pan and set on a baking sheet. Bake for about 1½ hours, covering the top lightly with foil if it begins to brown too quickly, until firm and set. Turn off the heat, leave the oven door ajar, and allow the cheesecake to cool in the oven. Carefully remove from the pan, transfer to a serving plate and chill for 2 hours before serving. Serve with light cream and fresh orange segments.

Ice box peanut chocolate torte

Family favorite

I made this one with the younger generation in mind, but I'm sure it'll be popular with everyone. It's fairly sweet so you won't want too much. Take care not to overfreeze the mixture as it will be difficult to cut.

Serves 8

4oz (125g) **milk chocolate**
⅔ cup (150g) **creamy peanut butter**
¼ cup (30g) **light brown sugar**
½ cup (125g) **full-fat cream cheese,
at room temperature**
1 cup (250ml) **whipping cream,
at room temperature**
8-in (20-cm) **round graham cracker
crumb crust (see tip below)**
1oz (30g) **white chocolate,** grated
1 tsp **cocoa powder**

Break the chocolate into pieces and place in a small heatproof bowl and melt over a saucepan of barely simmering water. Remove from the water and set aside.

Mix the peanut butter and sugar into the milk chocolate, and beat in the cream cheese. Whip the cream until just peaking and whisk into the mixture.

Spoon into the crumb crust. Smooth the top and freeze for 2 hours. Remove from the freezer and let stand for 15 minutes at room temperature before serving, sprinkled with grated white chocolate and a dusting of cocoa powder.

■ *To make your own crumb crust, mix 6oz (180g) crushed graham crackers with ¼ cup (60g) melted butter and press into a shallow base-lined 8-in (20-cm) round pie dish. Chill until required.*

Tropical fruit chocolate box gateau

Tropical fruit chocolate box gateau

Mouthwatering

The method for making a chocolate box can be used for round pans or smaller individual cases as well. Try to get an even thickness around the edges in order to support the filling.

Serves 8

10oz (300g) **semisweet chocolate**
Chocolate trifle sponge (see page 165)
4 Tbsp **coconut liqueur or syrup**
6oz (180g) **white chocolate**
⅔ cup (150ml) **heavy cream**
⅔ cup (150ml) **coconut milk**
Assorted prepared tropical fruit such as kiwi fruit, mango, pineapple, banana, star fruit, to decorate
Grated chocolate, to decorate

For the chocolate box, turn a 7-in (18-cm) square cake pan upside down. Mold a double layer of foil around the pan, pressing it around the corners. Carefully remove the foil and turn the pan right side up. Carefully press the foil "box" into the pan, making the foil as smooth as possible. Place a small piece of sticky tape at the top of the middle of each side, at the very edge of the foil, and fold over the edge to secure the foil to the pan. Place in the freezer for 20 minutes.

Break the semisweet chocolate into pieces and place in a heatproof bowl over a pan of barely simmering water until melted. Remove from the water.

Pour the hot chocolate into the foil-lined pan. Working quickly, tilt the pan to coat the bottom and the sides – you might want to wear gloves to do this as the pan will be very cold. Using a small spatula, spread the chocolate evenly right to the edges of the foil (do not cover the sticky tape), smoothing it into the corners. Chill in the fridge until set.

When the chocolate case is completely set, remove the sticky tape, carefully pull out the foil lining and peel it away from the chocolate. Put the chocolate box on a board. Trim the sponge to fit inside the chocolate box and carefully lower it into the bottom. Spoon the liqueur or syrup over the sponge. Chill until required.

Melt the white chocolate as above and set aside. Whip the cream until just peaking and then whisk in the coconut milk. Fold in the melted white chocolate and then spoon on top of the sponge. Smooth off the top and chill for at least 2 hours until firm.

To serve, decorate the top with a selection of tropical fruit and sprinkle with grated chocolate.

Sweets & treats

I had lots of fun with this section of the book and it made me realize how easy it can be to make sweets. You don't have to worry about sugar thermometers with these recipes, and you'll still achieve perfectly good results.

As well as the classic sweets like fudge, honeycomb and truffles, I've experimented with more exotic ones. Take a look at the Connoisseur truffles on page 140 to see what I mean. You'll have fun trying them out on your friends – I was amazed at how well these atypical flavors go with bitter chocolate – and perhaps you'll be inspired to try other flavors for yourself.

When I was a child, I used to make a refrigerated chocolate cake with my mom. It consisted of crushed graham crackers bound together with syrup, melted butter and melted chocolate, and set in a square cake pan. Not very healthy, but good as a treat once in a while. I've put in a couple of similar recipes: the Jumble slice for the kids – they can add anything they want to this – and the Chocolate "salami" for the grown ups – an Italian sweetmeat traditionally served with after-dinner coffee. Happy melting!

Connoisseur chocolate truffles

Contemporary

Several of the leading chefs and chocolatiers have experimented with different flavors that go with the darkest of chocolates. Here are two exciting flavors you might like to try on your friends.

Makes 30

2 **Thai red chilies or a** small bunch fresh basil
½ cup (100ml) **heavy cream**
¼ stick (30g) **unsalted butter**
6oz (180g) **85% cocoa bitter chocolate**
7oz (200g) **semisweet chocolate**
Small bitter Chocolate curls (see page 23), to decorate

First prepare either the chili or the basil. For the chili: cut in half and carefully scrape out the seeds. Roughly chop the flesh and place in a bowl. For the basil: wash and pat dry, rip up the leaves and stalk and place in a bowl.

Pour the cream into a small saucepan and add the butter. Heat gently to melt the butter and then pour this over your chosen flavoring and set aside to infuse until cool.

Break the bitter chocolate into small pieces and place in a heatproof bowl over a pan of barely simmering water. Allow to melt then remove from the water. Strain the infused cream onto the melted chocolate and mix well. Allow to cool until thick and fudgey. Note: If allowed to set, this mixture will be too hard to pipe.

Meanwhile, melt the semisweet chocolate as above and remove from the water. Drop small teaspoonfuls of the semisweet chocolate neatly on a large tray or board lined with baking parchment, and spread lightly to form discs about 1½in (4cm) in diameter. Chill until set.

Transfer the chocolate "fudge" to a piping bag fitted with a ½in (1cm) star nozzle. Pipe a swirl on top of each chocolate disc and chill for at least 30 minutes before serving. Decorate each with a chocolate curl.

Connoisseur chocolate truffles

No-fuss chocolate and coconut fudge

Easy peasy

Fudge-making can be quite difficult if you don't have a sugar thermometer, but this recipe doesn't need one. You'll end up with a sugary, dense texture that's absolutely delicious.

Makes 64 pieces

1lb (500g) **milk chocolate**
14-oz (397-g) **can condensed milk**
3 cups (250g) **unsweetened desiccated coconut**
½ tsp **ground allspice or cinnamon**
1 tsp **vanilla extract**

Grease and line an 8-in (20-cm) square cake pan with baking parchment. Break the chocolate into small pieces and place in a large heatproof bowl. Pour over the condensed milk and set over a bowl of barely simmering water. Allow to melt then remove from the water and stir until smooth and thick.

Mix in the coconut, spice and vanilla extract – the mixture will be very thick. Transfer to the prepared pan, smooth the surface and allow to cool completely. Chill for at least 2 hours until set. Carefully pull out from the pan using the baking parchment and, using a large sharp knife, cut into 64 squares. Store in an airtight container between layers of wax paper and keep in the fridge.

Christmas pudding truffles

Fruity

Let the children help you make these truffles; they can give them as festive treats to their friends. Add a tablespoon or two of rum or brandy for a grown-up version.

Makes 15

½ cup (100g) **semisweet chocolate chips**

8oz (250g) **fruit cake**

Generous ½ cup (100g) **no-need-to-soak dried figs**

1 tsp **pudding spice**

Scant ½ cup (60g) **white chocolate chips**

Tubes of red and green ready-made piping icing or colored fondant, to decorate

Place the semisweet chocolate chips in a heatproof bowl over a pan of barely simmering water until melted. Remove from the water and set aside.

Put the fruit cake in a blender or food processor with the figs and spice and blend for a few seconds to form a thick paste.

Mix the paste into the melted semisweet chocolate, allow to cool and then cover and chill for 30 minutes.

Form the chilled mixture into 15 balls and place on a board. Melt the white chocolate as above and spoon a little on top of each ball to resemble brandy sauce. Chill for a further 30 minutes until set.

Either pipe holly leaves and berry shapes onto each truffle or make them with fondant and place on top. Put each truffle in a petit four case to serve.

Chocolate mint crisps

Sparkly

Pretty little discs of crispy mint chocolate – they look lovely presented in gift-bags and given as a present. Enjoy with a cup of coffee.

Makes 24

½ cup (125g) **granulated sugar**
½ cup (125ml) **cold water**
2 tsp **peppermint extract**
8oz (250g) **semisweet chocolate**
Edible silver dragees, to decorate

Put the sugar in a small saucepan with the water. Heat gently, stirring, until the sugar dissolves, then bring to a boil and cook, without stirring, for about 8 minutes until thick and syrupy and just beginning to color – try not to brown the mixture. Remove from the heat and quickly stir in 1 tsp peppermint extract, whisking well. Pour onto a baking sheet lined with baking parchment and tap against the work surface to spread out evenly. Allow to set.

When it is cold, break the minty sugar into small pieces and place in a bowl. Crush with the end of a rolling pin.

Break the chocolate into small pieces and place in a large heatproof bowl and set over a bowl of barely simmering water. Allow to melt then remove from the water and cool for 10 minutes.

Stir the crushed minty sugar and remaining peppermint extract into the melted chocolate and drop teaspoonfuls of the mixture onto baking sheets lined with baking parchment, smoothing each portion into a round disc. Sprinkle over a few silver dragees before the chocolate sets.

Allow to cool then chill for 1 hour. Peel the sweets off the paper and store in an airtight container between layers of wax paper.

Chocolate mint crisps

Chocolate-covered honeycomb

Chocolate-covered honeycomb

Crisp

I love honeycomb – its crunchy yet chewy texture makes it a very satisfying sweet. Crushed honeycomb can make an interesting topping for ice cream and other chilled desserts.

Makes approx. 36 pieces (depending on size)

⅔ cup (150g) **granulated sugar**
2 Tbsp **corn syrup**
2 Tbsp **set honey**
2 tsp **baking soda**
14oz (400g) **milk chocolate**

Grease and line a 7-in (18-cm) square cake pan with baking parchment. Put the sugar in a large saucepan with the syrup and honey. Heat gently, stirring, until the sugar dissolves. Bring to a boil and cook, without stirring, for about 3 minutes until the mixture foams and turns a deep, golden caramel.

Remove from the heat and quickly stir in the baking soda. The mixture will immediately foam and bubble up in the saucepan, so quickly pour it into the prepared pan while still foaming. Set aside to cool.

When the honeycomb has set, carefully remove from the pan and peel away the paper. Cut into pieces using a large sharp knife – the honeycomb will shatter so you will end up with different sized and shaped pieces. Arrange the pieces, keeping them spaced apart, on a board lined with baking parchment and set aside.

Break the chocolate into small pieces and place in a large heatproof bowl and set over a pan of barely simmering water. Allow to melt then remove from the water and cool for 20 minutes.

Using small tongs or two forks, carefully dip the honeycomb pieces into the chocolate to cover them and place back on the parchment. Stand in a cool place to set – refrigerate only if the air temperature is warm and even then, chill for a short time, about 30 minutes, to set the chocolate; after this time the honeycomb may start to dissolve. Any small smashed pieces can be tossed into the remaining melted chocolate and set to make honeycomb clusters.

Peel the sweets off the parchment and store in an airtight container between layers of wax paper.

Chocolate marzipan slice

Almondy

Homemade marzipan is delicious. It's very easy to make and tastes much richer than anything bought from the store.

Makes 16 slices

1½ cups (200g) **ground almonds**
½ cup (125g) **superfine sugar**
1 Tbsp **cocoa powder**
1 tsp **good-quality vanilla extract**
Few drops **pink food coloring**
1 tsp **rose water**
Approx. 5 Tbsp **plain Sugar syrup**
   (see page 158)
Confectioner's sugar, to dust
4oz (125g) **semisweet chocolate**

Put the ground almonds in a bowl with the superfine sugar and mix together. Divide this mix among three small bowls. Stir the cocoa powder into one, the vanilla into another and add a few drops of pink food coloring and the rose water to the third bowl. Bind each together with sufficient Sugar syrup to form a firm pliable paste.

Dust your hands with confectioner's sugar. Roll each piece into a sausage shape approximately 7in (18cm) long and 1in (2.5cm) wide. Lay the pieces neatly one on top of the other, then press gently together to make a thickness of about 1½in (4cm). Wrap in baking parchment and pat gently to square off the sides. Chill until required.

Break the chocolate into small pieces, place in a heatproof bowl and set over a pan of barely simmering water. Allow to melt then remove the bowl from the water.

Spread the top of the marzipan with chocolate and chill for 10 minutes until set. Turn the marzipan over, and then spread one side with chocolate and chill until set. Conpanue in this way until the marzipan is covered. Chill until set.

To serve, dip a large, sharp knife in hot, boiled water, dry the blade and use to cut into thin slices.

■ *Serve as a sweet treat with coffee or after-dinner liqueur.*

Chocolate and coconut popsicles

Tropical

When the heat's on, chill out with this sweet chocolatey popsicle. They're easy to make and yummy to eat – you'll hardly be able to wait for them to freeze.

Makes 8

½ **quantity chocolate sugar syrup**
   (see page 158), cooled
Scant 1 cup (200ml) **canned coconut**
   milk
2oz (60g) **milk chocolate**
1 Tbsp **chocolate sprinkles**
   (vermicelli)
1 Tbsp **unsweetened desiccated**
   coconut, toasted

Mix the chocolate syrup and coconut milk together and divide among eight 4-Tbsp (60-ml) plastic popsicle molds – if you don't have special molds, you could use yogurt cups or other small dessert cartons instead. Take care not to over-fill the molds, because the mixture will expand during freezing. Place in the freezer for at least 4 hours until frozen solid – if you are not using molds, you'll need to push wooden popsicle sticks in to the middle of the popsicle mixture just as it starts to freeze. Once the popsicles have frozen, dip in hot water for a few seconds then carefully push out from the molds. Place the popsicles back in the freezer on a board lined with baking parchment.

Break the chocolate into pieces and place in a heatproof bowl over a pan of gently simmering water. Allow to melt, then remove from the water and set aside to cool for 10 minutes. Lightly drizzle the melted chocolate evenly over the popsicles and then immediately sprinkle with a few chocolate strands or toasted coconut before the chocolate sets. Either serve immediately or put back in the freezer until you are ready to eat them.

■ *For adults add 4 Tbsp white rum or coconut liqueur to the mixture before freezing.*

Jumble slice

Jumble slice

Allsorts

You can put just about anything in one of these melted chocolate mixtures. Try different types of dried or glacé fruits, and for a less sweet version, use continental semisweet chocolate.

Serves 12

1¼ sticks (150g) **unsalted butter**
1lb (500g) **milk chocolate,**
   broken into small pieces
6oz (180g) **chocolate chip cookies,**
   crushed into small pieces
¼ cup (60g) **glacé cherries,** chopped
⅓ cup (60g) **seedless raisins**
½ cup (60g) **mini marshmallows**
½ cup (125g) **Whoppers® or
   honeycomb (see page 145),** lightly
   crushed

Line a 4½-cup (500-g) loaf pan with clear food wrap. Place the butter and chocolate in a saucepan over a very low heat, stirring occasionally, until melted. Set aside for 10 minutes.

Meanwhile put the remaining ingredients together in a mixing bowl and stir until well combined.

Pour the melted chocolate over the dry mixture and stir well, making sure that all the pieces are thoroughly coated. Transfer to the prepared pan, press down well, cover loosely and chill for at least 2 hours until firm and set.

Remove from the pan and discard the food wrap. Using a large sharp knife, cut into 12 slices to serve. Keep refrigerated.

Salame al cioccolato

Chocolate "salami"

This might sound a little strange at first, but rest assured it's got nothing to do with meat. It is a very rich Italian confection traditionally served at the end of a meal with coffee and liqueur.

Serves 16

8oz (250g) **70% cocoa bitter chocolate**

1¼ sticks (180g) **unsalted butter,** cut into pieces

½ cup (60g) **toasted filberts,** very finely chopped or ground

¼ cup (30g) **candied citrus peel,** very finely chopped

6oz (180g) **crisp amaretti biscuits or almond macaroons,** finely crushed

¼ cup (30g) **ground almonds**

1¼ cups (15g) **confectioner's sugar**

Break the chocolate into small pieces and place in a large heatproof bowl with the butter. Set over a pan of barely simmering water. Allow to melt then remove from the water and cool for 10 minutes.

Stir the filberts, citrus peel and crushed biscuits into the chocolate and mix well. Leave in a cool place for about 30 minutes to firm up, but not set completely.

Turn the firm chocolate mixture onto a large sheet of baking parchment and form into a salami shape about 10in (25cm) long, with tapering ends. Wrap well in the parchment and chill for at least 4 hours until solid.

Mix the ground almonds and confectioner's sugar together and sift evenly over a sheet of baking parchment to cover an area the same length as the "salami." Unwrap the salami and roll evenly in the sweet almond mixture to coat. Let stand for 1 hour before slicing with a large knife, to serve.

Salame al cioccolato

Hot chocolate sandwich

Hot chocolate sandwich

Comfort food

If you need a sweet fix then here's the snack for you. Sliced strawberries, mashed raspberries or sliced mango would also be delicious fillings instead of banana.

Serves 1

2 slices **Pane al cioccolato (see page 94), brioche or other sweet bread, approx. ½-in (1-cm) thick**
¼ stick (30g) **unsalted butter,** softened
2 Tbsp **Chocolate spread (see page 166)**
1 **large banana,** mashed
2 Tbsp **milk chocolate,** grated

Thickly butter the bread and place buttered side down on a board lined with baking parchment. Spread the unbuttered sides with chocolate spread.

On one slice, carefully spread the mashed banana and sprinkle with the grated chocolate. Peel the other slice of bread off the parchment and gently press, chocolate side down, on top to make a sandwich.

Heat a nonstick ridged griddle or frying pan until hot, and press the sandwich onto the pan for about 2 minutes. Turn over and cook for a further 2 minutes until golden and lightly charred. Drain and serve immediately.

■ *Excellent with Chocolate cream sauce (see page 159) for extra indulgence!*

Chocolate ice cream sponge

Chiller

If you don't have much time, this dessert can be easily put together using ready-made ingredients. I prefer the mixture of white chocolate with blueberries, but you could try other combinations.

Serves 6

1 **quantity White chocolate ice cream (see page 120) or** 2¼ cups (500g) **ready-made, good-quality vanilla ice cream**
Chocolate trifle sponge (see page 165) or 7-in (19-cm) ready-made shallow square chocolate cake
⅔ cup (150g) **blueberries**
1oz (30g) **white chocolate**
1 tsp **cocoa powder**

Remove the ice cream from the freezer and stand at room temperature until it starts to soften – try to avoid it melting too much.

Meanwhile, line a deep 4½-cup (500-g) loaf pan with clear food wrap. Trim the sponge to fit snugly in the bottom of the pan. Cut another piece to fit the top and set aside.

Beat the ice cream to break it up and gently fold in the blueberries. Pack on top of the sponge base and top with the other piece of sponge, pushing down gently. Cover with clear food wrap and freeze for at least 2 hours.

To serve, melt the white chocolate (see page 21). Carefully remove the ice-cream sponge from the pan and peel off the food wrap. Drizzle with the white chocolate and dust with cocoa to serve.

■ *If you want to use other fruits in the dessert, make sure you use other berries or cut larger fruit into small pieces. You could use ready-frozen berries; just crush the bigger pieces with a rolling pin before mixing with the ice cream.*

Chocolate ice cream sponge

Accompaniments & quick recipes

Chocolate sugar syrup

Makes approx. 2½ cups (600ml)

2 cups (350g) **superfine sugar**
2½ cups (600ml) **cold water**
1 Tbsp **cocoa powder**

Place the sugar in a saucepan and pour in the water. Heat, stirring, until the sugar dissolves. Raise the heat and bring to a boil. Simmer, without stirring, for 10 minutes. Remove from the heat. Sift in the cocoa powder and whisk well. Set aside to cool.

■ *For a coffee sugar syrup, dissolve 2 tsp instant coffee granules in 1 Tbsp hot, boiled water and stir into the hot syrup. For a plain sugar syrup, simply omit the cocoa powder and allow to cool.*

Coffee cream sauce

Makes approx. 1¼ cups (300ml)

½ stick (60g) **unsalted butter**
½ cup (125g) **superfine sugar**
½ cup (125g) **corn syrup**
2 tsp **instant coffee granules** dissolved in 1 Tbsp hot, boiled water
⅔ cup (150ml) **heavy cream**

Place the butter, sugar and syrup in a saucepan and heat gently, stirring, until melted and the sugar dissolves. Stir in the coffee and cream and reheat until hot – do not allow to boil. Serve hot or cold.

Chocolate cream sauce

Makes approx. 1¼ cups (300ml)

6oz (180g) **semisweet chocolate,**
   broken into pieces
1 Tbsp (15g) **unsalted butter**
6 Tbsp **heavy cream**
3 Tbsp **corn syrup**
Few drops **vanilla extract**

Put all the ingredients except the vanilla extract in a small heatproof bowl. Set the bowl over a pan of gently simmering water, and heat slowly, stirring occasionally, until all the ingredients have melted together and the sauce is warm. Add a few drops of vanilla extract before serving. Serve warm – the sauce will harden on cooling.

■ *For a bitter chocolate sauce, use unsweetened chocolate. For milk and white chocolate sauces, melt equal quantities of chocolate to heavy cream – you will not need to add the corn syrup to either sauce.*

Chocolate custard sauce

Makes approx. 2½ cups (600ml)

4 level Tbsp **cornstarch**
1 Tbsp **cocoa powder**
2½ cups (600ml) **whole milk**
3 Tbsp **superfine sugar**
2 **egg yolks**
Few drops **vanilla extract**

In a saucepan, blend the cornstarch and cocoa powder with a little of the milk to make a smooth paste. Stir in the sugar and remaining milk. Heat, stirring, until boiling and thick – you may find it easier to use a whisk to help keep the mixture smooth. Cook for 2 minutes.

Remove from the heat and cool for 10 minutes. Stir in the egg yolks and return to the heat. Cook through for 3 minutes, stirring, but without boiling. Add vanilla to taste. To use cold, pour into a heatproof bowl and cover the surface with wax paper to prevent a skin forming. Allow to cool before covering and chilling until required.

■ *For a thicker pouring custard, use 1 Tbsp more of cornstarch. Omit the cocoa powder for a plain custard.*

Fruit sauce (raspberry and mango flavors)

Makes approx. 2¼ cups (550ml)

½ quantity plain Sugar syrup (see page 158)
1 cup (250g) **fresh raspberries,** washed and prepared
or 1 **large ripe mango,** stoned, peeled and chopped
1–2 Tbsp freshly squeezed **lemon or lime juice**

Make the syrup and add your chosen fruit to the syrup before it cools.

Once cold, transfer to a blender or food processor and blend for a few seconds until smooth. Strain through a nylon sieve to make a smooth sauce. Add lemon or lime juice to taste. Cover and chill until required.

Chocolate pastry

Makes 9-in (23-cm) pastry shell or
   12 x tartlet pans

1 cup (125g) **all-purpose flour**
1 Tbsp **cocoa powder**
Pinch **of salt**
¼ cup (60g) **superfine sugar**
½ stick (60g) **unsalted butter**
1 **egg yolk**
Few drops **of vanilla extract**
Approx. 1 Tbsp **whole milk**

Preheat the oven to 400°F (200°C). Sift the flour, cocoa, salt and sugar into a bowl, and rub in the butter to form a mixture that resembles fresh breadcrumbs. Mix in the egg yolk and vanilla extract and bring the mixture together adding milk if necessary, then knead gently to form a firm dough. Wrap and chill for 30 minutes.

Roll out the pastry thinly on a lightly-floured surface to fit a 9-in (23-cm) fluted loose-bottomed flan pan. The pastry is very short so you may find it easier to mold the pastry into the pan. Prick the base all over with a fork and bake in the oven for 15–20 minutes until set and firm to the touch.

White vanilla frosting

Makes enough to fill and cover
   8-in (20-cm) round, deep cake

2 cups (400g) **superfine sugar**
2 **egg whites (see note on page 4)**
Pinch **cream of tartar**
Pinch **salt**
1 tsp **vanilla extract**

Put all the ingredients except the vanilla extract in a heatproof bowl and whisk to make a thick paste. Place the bowl over a pan of gently simmering water and whisk for 6–7 minutes until thick and peaking.

Remove from the heat and whisk in the vanilla extract. Use this frosting immediately, before it begins to set.

Bitter chocolate fudge frosting

Makes enough to fill and cover
9-in (23-cm) round cake

10oz (300g) **unsweetened or 85%
(or above) cocoa bitter chocolate,
chopped**
½ stick (75g) **unsalted butter**
2 cups (300g) **confectioner's sugar**
¼ cup (75ml) **whole milk,** warm

Place the chocolate in a heatproof
bowl with butter and set over a pan of
gently simmering water and allow to
melt. Remove from the water and sift in
the confectioner's sugar. Gradually
whisk together, adding sufficient milk to
form a smooth, spreadable
consistency. Use quickly before it sets
and becomes difficult to spread.

Chocolate buttercream

Makes enough to fill and top
7-in (19-cm) round cake or top
12 muffins or fill jelly roll

¾ stick (90g) **unsalted butter,**
softened
1¼ cups (180g) **confectioner's sugar**
1 Tbsp **cocoa powder dissolved in
2 Tbsp boiled water,** cooled

Put the butter in a bowl and gradually
sift in the confectioner's sugar, beating
well between each addition, until
smooth and creamy. Stir in the
chocolate liquid and beat to soften the
mixture to a spreadable consistency.

■ *Add a few drops of vanilla extract or ½ tsp
grated orange rind, if liked, or replace 1 tsp
cocoa powder with 1 tsp instant coffee granules
for a mocha buttercream.*

Chocolate glacé icing

Makes enough to cover 10–12 cupcakes or muffins

1¼ cups (180g) **confectioner's sugar**
1 Tbsp **cocoa powder**
Approx. 5–6 tsp **warm, boiled water**

Sift the confectioner's sugar and cocoa into a bowl and gradually add sufficient water to make a smooth spreadable icing.

■ *Add a few drops of vanilla extract for extra flavor. Other flavors to add are peppermint extract, 1 tsp instant coffee granules dissolved in the water or ½ tsp finely grated orange rind.*

Glossy chocolate cream

Makes enough to cover 10-in (25-cm) round cake

7oz (200g) **semisweet chocolate, broken into pieces**
1 cup (250ml) **heavy cream, at room temperature**

Place the chocolate pieces in a heatproof bowl over a pan of gently simmering water and allow to melt. Remove from the water and set aside to cool until slightly warm – about 30 minutes.

While whisking the chocolate, gradually pour in the cream, whisking until thickly whipped and glossy. The mixture is now ready for spreading or piping. Once chilled the mixture will set firm.

■ *The cocoa content of the chocolate used will determine the sweetness of the chocolate cream, so choose a chocolate according to taste. This recipe also works with milk and white chocolate.*

Chocolate fondue

Serves 6

8oz (250g) **semisweet chocolate,**
  broken into pieces
1 cup (250ml) **heavy cream**
4 Tbsp **dark rum or** freshly squeezed
  orange juice
2 Tbsp **dark brown sugar**

Place the chocolate in a fondue pot or
small saucepan. Pour in the cream,
rum or juice, and add the sugar.

Place over a gentle heat, and cook,
stirring, until melted and well blended.
Either transfer to the fondue stand and
keep warm over the lit spirit burner, or
warm over a low heat on the stove
when required to serve.

■ *The cocoa content of the chocolate used will*
determine the sweetness of the chocolate
cream, so choose a chocolate according to
taste. This recipe also works with milk and white
chocolate, but you will not need to add the
sugar.

Rich hot chocolate drink

Serves 1

1oz (30g) **semisweet chocolate,**
  grated
Scant 1 cup (200ml) **whole milk**
2 **small cinnamon sticks**
1 **strip pared orange rind**
2 Tbsp **milk Chocolate spread**
  (see page 166)

Put the grated chocolate in a small
saucepan and pour over the milk. Add
one cinnamon stick and orange rind.
Heat very gently until the chocolate
melts, then stir in the Chocolate spread
and heat until melted. Bring to just
below boiling and turn off the heat. Let
stand for 5 minutes before straining
into a mug. Serve with a cinnamon
stick as a stirrer.

White chocolate toddy

Serves 1

2oz (60g) **white chocolate, grated**
2 Tbsp **heavy cream**
¾ cup (180ml) **whole milk**
¼ tsp **ground nutmeg**
Few drops **vanilla extract**

Put the grated chocolate in a small saucepan and pour over the cream and milk. Add half the nutmeg. Heat very gently, without boiling, until the chocolate melts. Continue to heat until piping hot but not boiling. Remove from the heat and add a few drops of vanilla extract. Pour into a mug and serve sprinkled with the remaining nutmeg.

Chocolate trifle sponge

Makes enough sponge for a large trifle

2 **large eggs**
Generous ¼ cup (60g) **superfine sugar**
¼ cup (30g) **all-purpose flour**
2 Tbsp (15g) **cocoa powder**
2 tsp **cornstarch**
¼ stick (30g) **butter, melted**

Preheat the oven to 350°F (180°C). Grease and line with baking parchment an 8-in (20-cm) square cake pan. Put the eggs and sugar in a large clean bowl and set over a large bowl of hot water. Whisk until thick, pale and creamy – about 5 minutes. Remove from the bowl of water and continue to whisk for a further 3 minutes. You should be able to leave a trail from a spoon in the mixture when it is whisked sufficiently.

Sift in the flour, cocoa and cornstarch. Pour the melted butter around the edge of the mixture and carefully fold the mixture together using a large metal spoon. Pour into the prepared pan and bake in the oven for 20–25 minutes until well risen and just firm to the touch. Remove from the pan and cool on a wire rack.

Chocolate spread

Makes 1¼ cups (300g)

4oz (125g) **milk or semisweet chocolate,** broken into pieces
½ stick (60g) **unsalted butter**
3 Tbsp **corn syrup**
3 Tbsp **heavy cream**

Place all the ingredients in a saucepan and heat very gently, stirring, until melted together, then remove from the heat and allow to cool.

Transfer to a sealable container and store in the refrigerator for up to 2 weeks.

Chocolate and vanilla pinwheels

Makes 18

1 stick (125g) **butter, softened**
¼ cup (60g) **superfine sugar**
1 **egg,** beaten
1 tsp **vanilla extract**
1⅔ cups (200g) **all-purpose flour**
2 Tbsp (15g) **cocoa**

Cream the butter and sugar together until pale and creamy. Beat in the egg and vanilla. Sift in the flour and mix to form a soft dough. Wrap half the dough and chill until required.

Sift the cocoa over the remaining dough and mix in thoroughly. Wrap and chill for 1 hour.

On a lightly floured surface roll each dough to form an oblong 10 x 8 in (25 x 20cm), and place on top of each other. Roll up tightly from the short end. Wrap and chill for 30 minutes. Preheat the oven to 375°F (190°C). Trim away the ends of the roll and slice thinly to make 18 rounds. Place a little distance apart on baking sheets lined with baking parchment and bake for 10–12 minutes until pale golden and set. Transfer to a wire rack to cool.

Chocolate ginger snaps

Makes 24

½ stick (60g) **unsalted butter**
½ cup (60g) **unbleached granulated or demerara sugar**
¼ cup (60g) **corn syrup**
⅓ cup (45g) **all-purpose flour**
2 Tbsp (15g) **cocoa powder**
½ tsp **ground ginger**

Preheat the oven to 350°F (180°C). Line two large baking sheets with baking parchment. Put the butter, sugar and syrup into a saucepan and heat gently, stirring, until the butter melts and the sugar dissolves. Remove from the heat and cool for 10 minutes.

Sift in the flour, cocoa and ginger and mix well. Drop small teaspoonfuls of the mixture onto the baking sheets, spaced about 7.5cm (3in) apart. Bake for 7–8 minutes until bubbling and spread. Leave to cool on the sheets, then remove and store between layers of wax paper in an airtight container for up to 1 week.

Maple chocolate smoothie

Serves 2

2 scoops **Bitter chocolate ice cream** (see page 120)
1¼ cups (300ml) **whole milk**
2 Tbsp **maple syrup**
Few drops **vanilla extract**
2 scoops **Milk chocolate ice cream** (see page 120)
Chocolate cream sauce (see page 159), to drizzle
2 tsp **white chocolate**, grated

Put the Bitter chocolate ice cream, milk, maple syrup and a few drops vanilla extract in a blender and blend for a few seconds until smooth.

Immediately pour into two tall glasses. Add a scoop of Milk chocolate ice cream to each glass. Drizzle with sauce and sprinkle with grated chocolate. Serve immediately.

Nut brittle

Makes approx. 7oz (200g)

Scant 1 cup (180g) **granulated sugar**
½ cup (100ml) **cold water**
½ cup (60g) **unsalted roasted nuts
such as pecans, filberts, almonds
or peanuts,** chopped

Put the sugar in a saucepan with the water and heat gently until dissolved. Raise the heat and boil rapidly, without stirring, for 7–8 minutes until the syrup turns light golden brown. Remove from the heat and dip the base of the saucepan briefly in cold water to prevent the caramel from cooking further. Working quickly, pour prepared caramel onto an oiled baking sheet and scatter over chopped nuts. Allow to cool.

When cold, lightly crush with a rolling pin and use as shards to decorate desserts such as trifles or cream-topped pies; or crush finer and use to mix into creams for fillings.

Chocolate shortbread

Makes 24 fingers

2 sticks (250g) **butter,** softened
½ cup (125g) **unbleached superfine
sugar**
2¼ cups (320g) **all-purpose flour**
½ tsp **salt**
¼ cup (30g) **cocoa powder**

Preheat the oven to 325°F (160°C). In a bowl, beat the butter and sugar together until soft and creamy. Add the flour and salt and sift over the cocoa powder. Carefully mix together and then beat until well combined.

Press into a 7 x 11-in (18 x 28-cm) oblong cake pan. Prick all over with a fork and bake in the oven for about 1 hour until firm. Cut into 24 fingers while warm and allow to cool in the pan.

■ *Dredge with a little superfine sugar and a light dusting of cocoa powder to serve, if liked.*

Top chocolatiers of the world

With specialty chocolate shops and delicatessens selling homemade chocolates for our indulgence just about everywhere we turn these days, I thought it might be useful to list some of the most famous producers of the world's finest chocolate. It would be a very long list to include them all, so this is only a taster. You'll be able to add your own favorites as you develop your chocolate palate. MC means that they have been given the title master chocolatier.

Austria
Altman & Kühne
  www.feinspitz.com/ak/
L. Heiner
  www.heiner.co.at

Belgium
Mary
  www.marychoc.com
Wittamer
  www.wittamer.com

Canada
Bernard Callebaut
  www.bernardcallebaut.com

France
Jean-Paul Hévin (MC)
  www.jphevin.com
La Maison du Chocolat (MC)
  www.lamaisonduchocolat.com
Michel Chaudin (MC)
  149 Rue de l'Université, 75007 Paris
Pierre Hermé (MC)
  www.pierreherme.com
Richart (MC)
  www.richart-chocolates.com

Germany
Dreimeister
  www.dreimeister.de
Fassbender
  www.fassbender.de

Italy
Amedei
  www.amedei.it
De Bondt (MC)
  Via Turati 22 (Corte San Domenico)
  56125 Pisa, Italy

Luxembourg
Oberweis
  www.oberweis.lu

Spain
Baixas
  Calaf 9–11, 08021 Barcelona
Fransico Torreblanca
  www.torreblanca.net

Sweden
Hovby No 9
  www.hovbyno9.se
Robert E's Choklad
  www.robertes-choklad.com

Switzerland
Camille Bloch
  www.camillebloch.ch
Dudle
  Weggisgasse 34, Lucerne CH-6004,
  Switzerland

United Kingdom
L'Artisan du Chocolat
  www.artisanduchocolat.com
The Chocolate Society
  www.chocolate.co.uk
Plaisir du Chocolat
  www.plaisirduchocolat.com
Rococo
  www.rococochocolates.com

United States of America
Fran's Chocolates
  www.franschocolates.com
Michael Recchiuti
  www.recchiuti.com
 Richard Donnelly Fine Chocolates
  www.donnellychocolates.com
Woodhouse Chocolat
  www.woodhousechocolate.com

About the author

Kathryn Hawkins is an experienced food writer and food stylist. She has worked on several women's magazines as part of their full-time staff and, since 1992, as a freelancer. She also runs a guest house.

Kathryn enjoys using local produce and is passionate about the quality and freshness of food on her doorstep. She writes on a wide range of cooking subjects and has a particular interest in cakes and baking, regional dishes, and healthy eating.

In addition to writing, Kathryn has prepared food for hundreds of photographs in advertisements, on food packaging, menus, and in magazines and books; she also teaches privately on a variety of subjects.

Index